CHOICES

INTERMEDIATE WORKBOOK

with Audio CD

ROD FRICKER

WITH ONLINE SKILLS BY GAVIN DUDENEY AND NICKY HOCKLY

CONTENTS

TOPIC TALK - VOCABULARY

1 Look at the clues and find the words.

```
     ¹b u i l d i n g s
      ²l        d
   ³a           e
         ⁴l     n
            ⁵t
      ⁶m        i
      ⁷c        t
 ⁸c              y
```

1 Houses, towers and schools are all …
2 An area of natural land – countryside, beaches – is part of the …
3 People sing the national … on special days and at international sporting events
4 French, Italian and Polish are all …
5 Real Madrid, Inter Milan and Bayern Munich are famous football …
6 Folk, reggae and punk are three types of …
7 A … is a set of clothes that people wear on certain special occasions.
8 England is a …

2 Choose the correct answer.

1 Where are your family roots?
 a In the Russian Federation.
 b In the kitchen cupboard.
 c At home.
2 What do you love about your country?
 a I love my family and friends.
 b I love French fashion, Italian food and American films.
 c The great music and the people.
3 What kind of person are you?
 a I'm a student.
 b I'm Irish.
 c I'm quite easy-going.
4 What are you keen on?
 a I'm romantic.
 b I really like sport.
 c I'm too laid-back.
5 What are you proud of in your country?
 a Our traditions and culture.
 b I'm very shy.
 c I'm not into tattoos.

3 Complete the text with the correct words. You can see the first letter of each word.

I live in Chicago in the USA but my ¹r<u>oots</u>____ are in Ireland. My great-grandfather came to the USA in 1904 and I'm very ²p_____ of my Irish blood. One ³t_____ that I love about Ireland are the people. Irish people are very friendly and talkative.

I'm an easy-going ⁴k_____ of person but I'm a ⁵b_____ too laid-back at times. That's what my teachers say! I'm passionate ⁶a_____ food. That's my great love. I can cook very well and I love trying new things. It's funny but, although I'm Irish, I'm not very ⁷k_____ on Irish food. I prefer Chinese and Indian food. I'm not ⁸i_____ sports. I have to play baseball and American football at school but I don't like them.

4 Complete the factfile about Jamaica with the words below.

Climate ~~Country~~ Flag Food Landmarks Landscape Language Music National anthem National costume People Wildlife

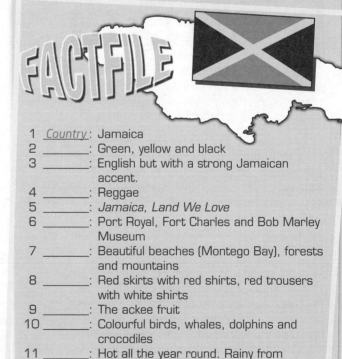

1 <u>Country</u> : Jamaica
2 _____ : Green, yellow and black
3 _____ : English but with a strong Jamaican accent.
4 _____ : Reggae
5 _____ : *Jamaica, Land We Love*
6 _____ : Port Royal, Fort Charles and Bob Marley Museum
7 _____ : Beautiful beaches (Montego Bay), forests and mountains
8 _____ : Red skirts with red shirts, red trousers with white shirts
9 _____ : The ackee fruit
10 _____ : Colourful birds, whales, dolphins and crocodiles
11 _____ : Hot all the year round. Rainy from May – November
12 _____ : Usain Bolt, Bob Marley and Grace Jones

1 Read the text about different identities in Great Britain and match the people to the areas and cities (paragraphs 1-6) that they come from.

a Brummies _3_

b The Cornish ___

c Geordies ___

d Scousers ___

e Tykes ___

f The Welsh ___

2 Read the text again. Match the headings (A-G) with the paragraphs (1-6). There is one extra heading.

A Almost a country

B Musical people

C Relaxed ... and great landscape

D Roots from across the sea

E Good people to go out with

F Different opinions about the accent

G Quiet people

DIFFERENT IDENTITIES IN GREAT BRITAIN

Some people from Great Britain call themselves British, and some call themselves English, Scottish or Irish. Many, though, take their identity from a much smaller area. Here are some of them.

1 _B_ . Wales is a separate country from England and it has its own government and capital city, Cardiff. It also has two official languages: English and Welsh. Although most people in the country speak Welsh as their second language, in the north of the country English is some people's second language. The Welsh are famous for their beautiful singing voices and choirs. Even the language sounds like singing.

2 ___ . Cornwall is in the far south-west of England. Many Cornish people say that their roots go back to the Celts who came west thousands of years ago to escape from the Romans. In fact, this isn't actually true but it helps give the people their identity. The Cornish have their own flag and language as well as a political party that wants Cornwall to become a separate country. At the moment it isn't ... not quite.

3 ___ . In the centre of England is the city of Birmingham. Most people in Britain think the Brummie accent is the least attractive of all local accents. However, studies of foreigners found that they think the accent is musical and pleasant. The number of comedians from the area shows that the locals have a good sense of humour and it is also home to a number of heavy metal bands.

4 ___ . Yorkshire covers a large area of northern England and the people who live here are often named after the local accent, Tyke. The people of Yorkshire are generally easy-going. The landscape is absolutely beautiful. Perhaps the most famous symbol of Yorkshire is the Yorkshire pudding, which is not sweet but eaten with meat.

5 ___ . Scouse is not only an accent but also a food similar to goulash and made with beef or lamb. Scousers come from Liverpool on the north-west coast of England but a lot of Scousers have their roots in Ireland. They are proud of their humour and the young tend to be well-dressed.

6 ___ . In the far north-east of England is the city of Newcastle. For many years, the city was a normal, dirty, industrial city but it has changed. A brand-new arts centre and bridge have made the city a brighter, more exciting place. The local people, Geordies, have a reputation for being very talkative and enjoying a good nightlife.

3 **Read the text again. Are the sentences true (T) or false (F)?**

1 Some people speak Welsh as their first language. ___

2 Most Cornish people's roots are Celtic. ___

3 The Birmingham accent is disliked by many British people. ___

4 The most famous symbol of Yorkshire is a sweet pudding. ___

5 Scouse is also a goulash made with meat. ___

6 Newcastle has always been different to other industrial cities. ___

Word Builder Compound adjectives

4 **Complete the sentences with the words below.**

> back conscious dimensional dressed going
> ~~known~~ looking new off

1 Are there any famous Scousers? Yes, The Beatles are very well-_known_.

2 My brother is very easy-_____. In fact, he's a bit too laid-_____.

3 The singer in this group is very good-_____ but he's not very well-_____ – his jeans and T-shirt are awful!

4 We've got a brand-_____ television but we didn't get a 3D one, we chose an old-fashioned two-_____ television.

5 I'm not very fashion-_____ because I'm not very well-_____. I can't afford to buy the latest designer-label jeans.

Sentence Builder *like*

5 **Choose the correct words to complete the sentences.**

1 Scouse *is like/likes/like* goulash.

2 Most people in England *are like/like/look like* Yorkshire pudding.

3 The new bridge in Newcastle *likes/looks like/like* the old one.

4 There are many accents in England, *like/look like/likes* Cornish, Geordie, Scouse and Tyke.

5 My sister really *is like/likes/looks like* chatting online.

6 My cousin *is like/like/look like* her mum.

6 **Complete the questions with the correct form of *like*.**

1 What _does_ the Liver bird, the symbol of Liverpool, _____ _____? It looks a bit like an eagle.

2 What _____ Welsh people _____? Outside the cities, they're often quiet, and traditional.

3 _____ Scousers _____ Geordies? Yes, they are in some ways. They're both talkative and funny and they both like going out.

4 _____ British people _____ the Brummie accent? No, they don't but a lot of foreigners do.

5 Who _____ your brother _____ _____? He definitely looks like my dad. They are both tall with brown hair.

Writing

7 **Read the instructions below. Write a short description of a person.**

Choose a friend or a member of your family to describe. Mention:
- What/Who he/she looks like
- What/Who he/she is like
- What he/she likes doing and give examples where necessary

GRAMMAR
Present tenses

REMEMBER

Complete exercises A–C before you start this lesson.

A Choose the correct words to complete the sentences.

1 **A:** What music *do you like/are you liking*?
   B: *I enjoy/I'm enjoying* lots of different kinds of music.
2 **A:** Hello. You *don't usually catch/aren't usually catching* the bus to school.
   B: I know but my dad *works/is working* in London today. He left in the car at 6 a.m.
3 **A:** What *do you read/are you reading*?
   B: *I read/I'm reading* a book about Native Americans. I *love/I'm loving* finding out about their traditions.
4 **A:** Hey, there's John. Where *does he go/is he going*?
   B: *He goes/He's going* to the tennis club. *He's often going/He often goes* there.

B Complete the sentences with the Present Perfect form of the verbs in brackets.

A: [1] *Have your family lived* (your family live) in Australia for a long time?
B: Yes, they have. My mum [2] _____ (be) here since 1967 and my dad's parents came here from Italy in 1947.
A: [3] _____ (you ever visit) your Mum and Dad's old countries?
B: Yes and no. I [4] _____ (be) to Italy twice but I [5] _____ (not have) a chance to see my grandparent's home town yet. I [6] _____ (see) lots of photos, though, and I really want to go there next year.
A: [7] _____ (you buy) your tickets yet?
B: No. I haven't got any money but my dad [8] _____ (promise) to pay for the flight and I will stay with my granddad's nephew. I [9] _____ (not eat) real home-cooked Italian food so that will be great.

C Complete the answers with the verb in the correct form or a short answer.

A: How often do you write emails?
B: I usually [1] _____ *write* _____ one or two emails a day.
A: What are you writing at the moment?
B: I [2] _____ my blog.
A: Have you ever written a poem?
B: Yes, I [3] _____.
A: Does Amy like skiing?
B: Yes, she [4] _____.
A: How often does she go skiing?
B: She [5] _____ skiing every February.
A: Is she skiing at the moment?
B: No, she [6] _____.

1 * Complete the sentences with the verbs below.

are you doing   do you usually do   has become
have lived   have you done   ~~is watching~~
'm doing   watches   wears

1 My brother *is watching* TV at the moment.
2 My friend _____ a punk and now looks completely different.
3 What _____ on Saturday afternoons?
4 My sister always _____ black jeans.
5 My parents _____ in this house for twenty years.
6 I can't chat now, I _____ my homework.
7 My mum never _____ television.
8 _____ anything at the moment?
9 _____ your homework yet?

2 * Complete the answers in the same tense as the questions.

1 What is your sister doing at the moment?
   She *'s watching* TV.
2 How often does your mum visit your grandparents?
   She _____ them once a week.
3 Is your dad working this evening?
   No, he _____. He never works in the evenings.
4 Have you ever been to Venice?
   No, but I _____ to Rome.
5 How long have your parents had this car?
   They _____ it for ten years but it still goes well.
6 Does your mum tell you what you can and can't wear?
   No, but she _____ me what time I have to come home in the evening.
7 How often does your teacher give you homework?
   He usually _____ us homework twice a week.
8 What are you thinking about?
   I _____ about my date with Samantha next Friday.
9 Has Tom bought a new computer yet?
   No, he _____ but he _____ an MP3 player.

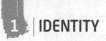

3 ** Six of the sentences below use the wrong tense. Find the incorrect sentences and correct them. Tick (✓) or (✗).

1 We live here for ten years. ✗
_____We have lived here for ten years._____

2 I don't want anything to eat at the moment. ☐
_____

3 My uncle's had a very interesting life. ☐
_____

4 I'm having these badges since about 2007. ☐
_____

5 Are you still studying German? ☐
_____

6 Are you belonging to an urban tribe? ☐
_____

7 Are you ever studying Italian? ☐
_____

8 Tim hasn't always been so fashion-conscious. ☐
_____

9 What do you think about at the moment? ☐
_____

10 I'm not having a favourite band at the moment. ☐
_____

4 *** Complete the sentences with the correct form of the verbs in brackets. Use the Present Simple, Present Continuous and Present Perfect in each text.

1 My family _have lived_ (live) in the USA for over a hundred years but my dad _____ (think) of himself as Swedish. At the moment, he _____ (visit) Stockholm to find his old family home.

2 I _____ (not know) who I really am. In my life, I _____ (be) a student, a punk rocker, a worker, a father and lots of other things. Now, I _____ (try) to work out which is the real me.

3 My dad _____ (just start) looking at our family tree. He _____ (want) to know where our family is from. At the moment, he _____ (read) about his great-great-great-great grandfather, a baker from Doncaster.

4 We _____ (do) a project at school at the moment on 'our identity'. So far, we _____ (spend) three lessons and some homework time on it and we still haven't finished. My friend, Elaine, _____ (not understand) why we're doing it but I think it's really interesting.

Grammar Alive Personal information

5 Use the cues to write questions and answers.

1 A: you often / speak English?
Do you often speak English?

B: No / not often speak / but sometimes read in English
No, I don't often speak English but I
sometimes read in English.

2 A: What / usually / use English for?
_____

B: sometimes read books in English / write a blog every week / at the moment – try to understand the words to a song by Jet.
_____
_____
_____

3 A: How many blogs / write / this month?
_____

B: write / three so far
_____

4 A: people / often leave comments about your blogs?
_____

B: Yes, my friend / always write / comments
_____

5 A: How often / you / play online games in English?
_____

B: Every day / but not read / the instructions.
_____

SKILLS
Listening

1 Complete the phrases with the correct verb: *be into, hang out, have* or *wear*.

1 _have_ long/short hair
2 _____ horror films
3 _____ at skate parks
4 _____ leather jackets
5 _____ baggy clothes
6 _____ a beard
7 _____ scruffy clothes
8 _____ in the town centre
9 _____ black make-up
10 _____ dyed hair
11 _____ indie and punk
12 _____ depressing music

2 Complete the sentences with the urban tribes below.

emo ~~geek~~ goth metal head punk skater trendy

1 I'm a/an _____geek_____. I love computers and spend most of my time playing online games.
2 I'm a/an _____. I've got a shaved head and a pierced nose. I wear scruffy clothes.
3 I'm a/an _____. I wear a leather jacket and a black T-shirt. I've got long hair and a beard.
4 I'm a/an _____. I wear dark clothes and I've dyed my hair black. I love emotional music.
5 I'm a/an _____. I love horror films and silver jewellery. I wear a lot of black make-up.
6 I'm a/an _____. I go clubbing every Friday and Saturday and wear fashionable clothes with designer labels.
7 I'm a/an _____. I wear baggy trousers and listen to punk and indie music. Oh, and I go to the skate park every weekend.

3 `1.2` Listen to ten short conversations. For each one, write *A* if the two people agree or *D* if they disagree.

1 _D_   4 ___   7 ___   10 ___
2 ___   5 ___   8 ___
3 ___   6 ___   9 ___

4 `1.2` Listen again and complete the conversations with the correct words.

1 **A:** I _think_ punks are dangerous.
   B: I _____. They just look dangerous.
2 **A:** I _____ old rock music.
   B: _____ _____ I. It's much better than modern music.
3 **A:** I _____ _____ wearing lots of make-up.
   B: _____ _____ I. It looks terrible.
4 **A:** _____ _____ horror films.
   B: _____ _____ _____.
5 **A:** I _____ _____ British teenagers look very fashionable.
   B: _____ _____. Most young people look really cool.
6 **A:** I _____ piercings.
   B: _____, _____. They're awful.
7 **A:** _____ _____ _____ fashionable clothes.
   B: Really? I _____.
8 **A:** I _____ _____ to go to the concert on Saturday.
   B: _____ _____. It's too expensive.
9 **A:** I'm _____ _____ of downloading music from the internet without paying.
   B: _____ _____. It's stealing.
10 **A:** _____ _____ _____ Reality TV shows.
   B: _____ _____ _____.

5 Write the replies using the instructions below.

1 **A:** I think they look a bit silly.
   B: (Agree with A. Use three words) _____.
2 **A:** I'm not into their clothes.
   B: (Agree with A. Use three words) _____.
3 **A:** I don't think we're a tribe.
   B: (Agree with A. Use two words) _____.
4 **A:** I just love urban tribes.
   B: (Agree with A. Use two words) _____.
5 **A:** I'm into their music.
   B: (Disagree with A. Use two words) _____.
6 **A:** I don't like those groups.
   B: (Disagree with A. Use two words) _____.

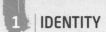

Check Your Progress 1

1 Identity. **Complete the sentences with the words below. There are two extra words.**

> anthem   into   climate   proud   flag   roots
> landscape   keen   labels   landmark

1 I think the music of our national _____ is a bit old-fashioned.
2 Clothes with designer _____ are a waste of money.
3 None of my friends are _____ on art.
4 The most famous _____ in our country is the castle on a hill in our capital city.
5 I hate our country's _____. It's always cold and rainy.
6 I'm _____ of my country and its history.
7 I'm not really _____ traditional dances and music.
8 The _____ in my country is beautiful.

/8

2 Compound adjectives **Match the words (1-6) with (a-j) to make compound adjectives. One word matches with three endings.**

1 easy-	___	**a**	dressed
2 good-	___	**b**	going
3 laid-	___	**c**	known
4 ready-	___	**d**	off
5 well -	___	**e**	looking
		f	back
		g	made

/5

3 **Complete the sentences with compound adjectives from Exercise 2.**

1 Not everyone can afford designer labels – we're not all as _____ as you are.
2 I know Ben's _____ but he doesn't have to keep looking at himself in the mirror.
3 I know you like to be _____ all the time but you don't have to wear a suit and tie to the beach!
4 These _____ meals are easy to cook but they have no flavour at all.
5 Dan likes wearing T-shirts with band logos on them but only bands which aren't _____. He's not interested in famous groups.

/5

4 Present tenses **Complete the dialogue with the correct form of the verbs below.**

> be (x 2)   have   like   look   not think   stand   try

A: So, you're an emo. Have you ever [1]_____ in any other urban tribes?
B: Oh, yes. I [2]_____ a punk and a goth.
A: So why are you an emo now?
B: I [3]_____ the clothes they wear. I think emos [4]_____ better than punks and goths.
A: What are you doing at the moment?
B: We [5]_____ to get tickets for an emo concert but, we [6]_____ at the back of a long queue. I [7]_____ we'll get any.
A: So, why don't you go home now?
B: We [8]_____ fun!

/8

5 Agreeing and disagreeing **Write the replies using the instructions below.**

1 **A:** I'm proud of my country.
   B: (Agree with A. Use three words) _____
2 **A:** I love our climate.
   B: (Disagree with A. Use two words) _____
3 **A:** I'm into jazz.
   B: (Disagree with A. Use two words) _____
4 **A:** I sing the national anthem on special days.
   B: (Agree with A. Use three words) _____

/4

TOTAL SCORE   /30

Module Diary

1 **Look at the objectives on page 5 in the Students' Book. Choose three and evaluate your learning.**

1 Now I can _____
   well / quite well / with problems.
2 Now I can _____
   well / quite well / with problems.
3 Now I can _____
   well / quite well / with problems.

2 **Look at your results. What language areas in this module do you need to study more?**

Sound Choice 1

1 **1.4** **Grammar - contractions** **Listen to the sentences and write the contractions. Then repeat the sentences.**

1 _I'm_   3 _____   5 _____
2 _____   4 _____   6 _____

2 **1.5** **Grammar - 3rd person -s** **Listen and write the words in the correct column depending on the sound of the final -s.**

/s/	/z/	/ɪz/
likes	_____	_____
_____	_____	_____
_____	_____	_____

3 **1.6** **Consonants** **Tick (✓) the words you hear.**

1	rude ☐	root ✓
2	glass ☐	class ☐
3	pack ☐	back ☐
4	tie ☐	die ☐
5	boat ☐	vote ☐
6	ice ☐	eyes ☐
7	niece ☐	knees ☐
8	cold ☐	gold ☐
9	bet ☐	vet ☐
10	buy ☐	pie ☐

4 **1.7** **Vowels** **Listen to the words. Tick (✓) the words you hear or write the word if it is different.**

1 feet ✓ _____
2 band ☐ _bend_
3 man ☐ _____
4 live ☐ _____
5 fan ☐ _____
6 land ☐ _____
7 cup ☐ _____

5 **1.8** **Spelling - silent letters** **Listen and write the words. Circle the silent letters.**

1 _badge_   4 _____   7 _____
2 _____   5 _____   8 _____
3 _____   6 _____   9 _____

6 **1.9** **Expressions - sentence stress** **Circle the word which has the main stress. Now listen to check your answers.**

1 So do I.	4 I do.	7 Me too.
2 I don't.	5 I'm not.	8 So am I.
3 Neither am I.	6 Me neither.	

7 **1.10** **Difficult words - word stress** **Listen to the words and match them to the correct stress pattern.**

Ooo	oOo	oOoo	ooOo	oooOo
_____	_____	_rebellious_	_____	_____
_____	_____	_____	_____	_____

8 **1.11** **Difficult words - Word stress** **Look at these compound words. Is the stress on the first or the second word? Underline the stressed word. Listen to check and repeat the words.**

1 hard-working	6 laid-back
2 easy-going	7 ready-made
3 brand-new	8 two-dimensional
4 fashion-conscious	9 well-dressed
5 good-looking	10 well-known

TOPIC TALK – VOCABULARY

1 Match the descriptions (1-8) with the events (a-h).

1 I remember when Michael Jackson died. _e_
2 My parents celebrated twenty years together with a trip to Paris. ___
3 I watched the running and swimming but nothing else. ___
4 My sister was born on 29 February 2005. ___
5 It was an exciting match which Liverpool won 2-0. ___
6 I invited ten friends to my house for my birthday. ___
7 Four days after my grandfather died, thirty people came to 'say goodbye'. ___
8 We got married in church and fifty people were there to watch us. ___

a A birth
b The Olympics
c A wedding
d A funeral
e A death
f A cup final
g An anniversary
h A party

2 Complete the text with the correct words. You can see the first letter of each word.

Here is the news:

■ People in the USA are still talking about yesterday's ¹e_lection_ of the first ever woman President.

■ There was a plane ²c_____ in Zaire yesterday. It happened during a storm.

■ A fire in Mexico City was caused by gas, not a terrorist ³a_____ say the police.

■ Workers at a nuclear power station in England have stopped a nuclear ⁴d_____ . People living near the power station are now able to return to their homes.

■ There has been three days of heavy rain in Pakistan. The ⁵f_____ there are the worst for twenty years.

■ There has been another large ⁶e_____ in Indonesia. Buildings fell down in the capital, Jakarta.

■ In Australia, a forest ⁷f_____ has destroyed about 10,000 kilometres of forests and it is still burning.

3 Complete the descriptions of the pictures with the correct words.

1 We _danced_ all night.

2 My mum and aunt _____ each other at the barbeque .

3 Andy _____ the only goal of the game.

4 Karen _____ the race in 11.41 seconds.

4 Complete the sentences with the phrases below.

it happened   best bit   earliest memories   it was great
~~special event~~   sporting memories

1 One _special event_ I remember, was my brother's wedding.
2 _____ because we all had a good time.
3 One of my best _____ was when my dad took me to see a cricket match.
4 The _____ was when the players held the cup up and we all went wild.
5 One of my _____ was a flood when I was about five.
6 When _____ we were driving home from my aunt's house.

GRAMMAR
Past Perfect

REMEMBER

Complete exercises A-B before you start this lesson.

A Complete the text with the Past Simple form of the verbs in brackets.

I ¹ ____had____ (have) a terrible time at the cinema last week. First of all, the bus ² _____ (be) late. I ³ _____ (get) off the bus about five minutes before the film ⁴ _____ (start) and I ⁵ _____ (run) to the cinema. Then I ⁶ _____ (fall) over and got a hole in my jeans! Luckily, I ⁷ _____ (not hurt) myself. In the cinema, I ⁸ _____ (buy) my ticket and some popcorn and I ⁹ _____ (go) in just in time. Unfortunately, I ¹⁰ _____ (not have) time to get to my seat before they ¹¹ _____ (switch) off the lights. In the dark, I ¹² _____ (stand) on someone's foot and ¹³ _____ (drop) my popcorn!

B Complete the dialogues with the Past Simple or the Past Continuous form of the verbs in brackets.

A: I ¹ _was cooking_ (cook) dinner, yesterday, when the electricity suddenly ² _____ (go) off.

B: What ³ _____ (cook)?

A: Eggs.

B: What ⁴ _____ (you do)?

A: I got out my gas cooker that I take camping and I cooked them on that.

A: My parents ⁵ _____ (drive) in the countryside, when a man ⁶ _____ (walk) in front of their car.

B: Where ⁷ _____ (they go)?

A: They ⁸ _____ (go) to a party.

B: ⁹ _____ (they stop)?

A: No, my mum screamed and my dad ¹⁰ _____ (drive) past him on the wrong side of the road.

1 * **Match the beginnings (1-6) with the endings (a-f).**

1 I felt sick because ... __c__
2 I couldn't buy the T-shirt because ... ____
3 My mum was angry because ... ____
4 The crowd went wild because ... ____
5 No one came to the party because ... ____
6 I failed my exams because ... ____

a I hadn't done the shopping for her.
b I hadn't studied the right topics.
c I had eaten too much cake.
d their team had won the cup.
e I had spent all my money on CDs.
f we had forgotten to send the invitations.

2 ** **Complete the sentences with the Past Perfect form of the verbs in brackets.**

1 The phone rang while Mark was cooking sausages on a barbecue. When he came back, they had ____all gone____ (all go). The other people at the party _____ (eat) them all.

2 We were driving along the motorway when, suddenly, we stopped. There were lots of cars and none of them were moving. Two cars _____ (crash) and the police _____ (close) the road so that an ambulance could come and take the injured people to hospital.

3 There was a forest fire near our house. Someone _____ (throw) away a cigarette. Because it _____ (not rain) for several weeks, everything was very dry and the fire started quickly.

4 We went to the Olympic Games swimming competition. My dad _____ (buy) tickets two years before but he _____ (not tell) us about them so it was a big surprise.

3 *** Choose the correct past tense to complete the text.

My best sporting memory wasn't a game at all. It ¹*happened/was happening/had happened* three years ago when my favourite team got to the cup final. My dad and I ²*were at/were going to/had been* to all our team's matches that year so decided to get tickets. When we asked at the club, they ³*sold/were selling/had sold* all the tickets already. We were disappointed but we ⁴*watched/were watching/had watched* it on television. It ⁵*finished/was finishing/had finished* 1–1 so the two teams had to play a second match the following Wednesday. We ⁶*still watched/were still watching/had still watched* television when my dad said: 'Let's go to the ground tomorrow and try to get some tickets.' We arrived at 7 a.m. but there was already a long queue. Some people ⁷*were/were being/had been* there since the evening before. Luckily, the sun ⁸*shone/was shining/had shone* and everyone was happy. While we ⁹*stood/were standing/had stood* there, someone gave me a scarf which I've still got. We finally got the tickets and ¹⁰*went/were going/had gone* to the match but I remember buying the tickets much more clearly.

4 *** Complete the sentences with the Past Continuous, Past Simple or Past Perfect form of the verbs below.

~~arrive~~   leave

When I ¹ *arrived* at Fiona's party, everyone
² _____ so I asked them why.

come   tell

One boy ³ _____ me that Fiona's parents
⁴ _____ back early.

not tell   tell

Fiona ⁵ _____ her parents about the party so they
⁶ _____ everyone to go home.

stop   walk

Luckily, while I ⁷ _____ to the bus stop, a friend's
father ⁸ _____ and gave me a lift home.

Grammar Alive Excuses and explanations

5 Complete the dialogue with the verbs below. There are three extra verbs.

bought   ~~Did you enjoy~~   didn't you buy   didn't you wear
disappeared   had disappeared   had it gone   had taken
hadn't you worn   was buying   was wearing

A: ¹*Did you enjoy* the party?
B: No, I didn't. Everyone there ² _____ fancy dress, except for me.
A: Why ³ _____ something to wear?
B: I did. I ⁴ _____ a great police officer's uniform.
A: So, why ⁵ _____ it?
B: Because, when I tried to find it, it ⁶ _____.
A: Where ⁷ _____?
B: My brother ⁸ _____ it and worn it to a different party.
A: That's terrible.

Listening

1 〔1.12〕 **Listen to a news item. While you listen, put the events in the order that they happened.**

1 A match was played in August. ___
2 They played Red Star Belgrade _1_
3 There was a minute's silence to remember the crash. ___
4 They flew to Munich. ___
5 Manchester United lost 2-1. ___
6 They crashed. ___
7 They beat Benfica 4-1. ___

2 〔1.12〕 **Listen again and choose the best answers.**

1 How many times had Manchester United won the English championship before the crash?
   a never   **c** twice
   b once   **d** three times
2 The Manchester United players had just flown from:
   a Manchester.   **c** Belgrade.
   b Munich.   **d** London.
3 The crash happened:
   a before they got to Munich.
   b when the plane was landing.
   c before they played the match.
   d as they tried to leave for London.
4 After the accident:
   a none of the players played again.
   b they had to get a new manager.
   c Manchester United didn't win again that year.
   d they finished ninth in the championship.
5 The idea for the fortieth anniversary came from:
   a the fans.   **c** the players.
   b the director. **d** Eric Cantona.
6 Why were people upset about the fortieth anniversary match?
   a It didn't take place in February.
   b The players and their families didn't get much money from it.
   c There wasn't a very big crowd.
   d They didn't like Eric Cantona.
7 At the fiftieth anniversary match, which of these things didn't happen?
   a The players wore old style football shirts.
   b The Manchester City crowd made a noise during the minute's silence.
   c A man played bagpipes in the stadium.
   d Manchester United lost the match.

Word Builder Multi-part verbs (1)

3 **Complete the sentences with the correct form of the verbs below. One sentence can be completed with two verbs.**

come out of   get on with   get together   go out
join in   kick-off   meet up   stand up

1 At three o'clock, the French _kicked off_ and the game started.
2 Two boys were fighting outside so our teacher _____ to stop them.
3 My brother _____ hospital after two weeks and we had a party to celebrate.
4 I've got a big family and we all _____ / _____ on our birthdays for a big party.
5 My cousin started singing and we all _____.
6 I was glad that my friends from home and my friends from school _____ each other so well.
7 All the fans _____ and cheered when the players appeared.

Sentence Builder *just*

4 **Match the sentences with the correct meanings of the word *just*: very recently, really/totally, only/simply.**

1 The game had just started when they scored the first goal. _very recently_
2 That card you sent me was just brilliant. _____
3 I'm sorry you fell over. I was just trying to get past you. _____
4 I'm not staying. I just wanted to say 'Happy Birthday'. _____
5 I had just left home when I realised I had forgotten my key. _____
6 The first goal was just amazing. _____

LESSON

6

GRAMMAR
used to and *would*

1 * **Look at the pictures and complete the sentences with the correct form of *used to* and the verbs in brackets.**

Simon, aged 10...

Simon, now...

1 Simon _used to play_ (play) football.

2 He _____ (be) a good player.

3 He _____ (score) a lot of goals.

4 He _____ (eat) unhealthy food.

5 He _____ (watch) too much TV.

6 He _____ (be) lazy.

2 ** **Look at the pictures and complete the text with the verbs below with *used to* and *would*. Where both are possible, use both forms.**

Melanie, aged 5...

Melanie, now...

get ~~always / have~~ not have ~~love~~ eat not go
not invite not wait open

Melanie ¹_always used to have/would always have_ big parties. She ²_____used to love_____ them.
She had lots of friend but she
³_____ any boys! She
⁴_____ any dinner on her
birthday but she ⁵_____ a lot
of cake.
She definitely ⁶_____to
restaurants on her birthday with just one
other person. She had too many friends! She
⁷_____ lots of presents and
she ⁸_____ them very quickly.
She ⁹_____ until the end of the
evening before opening them. She was too excited!

3 ** **Cross out the words which are wrong. Sometimes both words are correct.**

1 I *used to/~~would~~* live in a big city.

2 My grandmother *used to/would* look after us when our parents went out.

3 I *would/used to* help my grandmother make cakes.

4 I *used to/would* want a lot of pets.

5 Tim *wouldn't/didn't use to* understand anything our French teacher said.

6 My mum *wouldn't/didn't use to* let us watch television on school days.

7 The school bus driver *wouldn't/didn't use to* wait for us to sit down and we *would always/always used to* fall over when he drove off.

8 What *would you/did you use to* like doing most when you were young?

9 *Would your parents/Did your parents use to* tell you to write 'Thank you' letters to people who had given you presents?

4 *** **Complete the second sentence so that it has the same meaning as the first sentence. Use the word in capitals in your answer.**

1 I never opened the door when I was alone in the house.
(USE)
I _didn't use to open_ the door when I was alone in the house.

2 Did you switch off your bedroom light when your parents told you to?
(TO)
Did _____ your bedroom light when your parents told you to?

3 My friend Keith never said anything at parties.
(WOULDN'T)
My friend Keith _____ at parties.

4 I loved going to my grandparents' house when I was young.
(LOVE)
I _____ going to my grandparents' house when I was young.

5 When I watched frightening films, I always closed my eyes and put my fingers in my ears.
(WOULD)
When I watched frightening films, I _____ my eyes and put my fingers in my ears.

Workshop 1

Writing

1 You are in the USA and have been to an American friend's Thanksgiving dinner. Look at what happened and then complete sentences (1-6) using *before*, *after* or *while* + the *-ing* form of the verb.

- *I read about the history of Thanksgiving.*
- *I left home and travelled by bus.*
- *I waited for my friend's parents at the bus station. I bought some flowers for them.*
- *We waited for dinner. I helped to get the house ready.*
- *We ate.*
- *I felt really full.*
- *We watched the American Football on the television. We ate more cakes!*
- *I talked to my family in England on my friend's computer.*

1 _Before leaving_ home, I read about the history of Thanksgiving.

2 _____ for my friend's parents, I bought them some flowers.

3 _____ for dinner, I helped to get the house ready.

4 _____ dinner, I felt really full.

5 _____ the American football, we ate even more cakes.

6 _____ to bed, I talked to my family on my friend's computer.

2 You are going to write an email to a friend about the Thanksgiving dinner. Choose the most informal expressions to use in your email.

1 *Dear Mr Finch/Hi there, Steve*

2 *How are you?/ How's everything?*

3 The journey by bus was *terrible/a nightmare.*

4 I was completely *exhausted/wiped out* by the end of the evening.

5 I ate *a lot of/lots of* food.

6 *All the best/Yours*

3 Use the ideas from Exercises 1 and 2 to write your email in your notebook. Write between 120 and 150 words.

Speaking

1 **1.13** Put the replies below in the correct places in the conversation. Then listen to check.

> And then?   Amazing!   Oh no!   ~~Really?~~

A: A very lucky thing happened to me recently.

B: [1] _Really?_

A: Yes. I was going to a concert with some friends. We met up at a café on a busy road.

B: [2] _____

A: After saying hello, I looked at my watch and we decided to go to the concert hall. Just then, I looked in my pocket and realised I had lost the tickets and all my money.

B: [3] _____

A: Yes. So, we walked back the way I'd come and there they were on the ground with a £20 note. There were hundreds of people walking past and no one had seen them.

B: [4] _____

A: I know. I felt so happy, I couldn't believe it.

2 Choose the correct words to complete the dialogue.

A: It [1] *happened/worked* last summer. I was on holiday in Germany with some friends. We'd [2] *just/suddenly* got on a train and found some empty seats. It was quite cold and I [3] *had worn/was wearing* a blue and yellow football scarf.

B: And then, what happened?

A: [4] *Anyway/Suddenly*, some German football fans got on the train. They came up to me and started pointing.

B: Oh no!

A: I was quite surprised. I didn't know what they wanted, [5] *but then/eventually* my friend, who speaks some German, told me that they thought my scarf was for an old German team.

B: Really?

A: Yes, their local team, I forget who, had changed their colours a long time ago. No one had worn those colours for ages. So [6] *after/anyway*, then I took the scarf off and showed it to them. It had 'Oxford United' on it. [7] *After/Just* that, they were very friendly. They started talking to us in English. They were very funny. One of them took my scarf and opened the window. When we came to a station, he shouted 'Oxford' as loudly as he could.

B: No!

A: Yes, the people at the station looked very surprised.

B: Then what happened?

A: [8] *Eventually/But then* they got off and we saw some other football fans. I took my scarf off and put it in my bag before they got on. We'd had a good time but I wanted a rest!

Check Your Progress 2

1 Memories **Complete the text with the correct words. You can see the first letter of each word.**

The ¹b_____ of a new baby is always a special time but it's not the only time that families get together. We ²c_____ birthdays, we go to ³w_____ and hope that the new husband and wife will be happy together. Even ⁴f_____ are a chance for families to meet up and remember the past. Although ⁵d_____ is always sad, the meeting doesn't have to be. One celebration that isn't usually a big event is a ⁶w_____ a_____. Often the husband and wife just go for a meal together or for a weekend away in a romantic city.

/6

2 Mulit-part verbs **Complete the sentences with the correct words.**

1 When my uncle came _____ of prison, my family helped him to find somewhere to live and to get a job.

2 My friends and I always meet _____ in the town centre on Saturdays.

3 Do you get _____ well with your neighbours?

4 When the police arrived, my dad went _____ to talk to them.

5 We all stood _____ and cheered when the headmaster gave us a day off.

6 I didn't want to dance but, when everyone else started, I felt I had to join _____.

/6

3 Past simple, Past continuous, Past Perfect, used to and would **Complete the text with the correct form of the verbs in brackets**

When Elvis Presley ¹_____ (die) my mum ²_____ (listen) to the radio. Suddenly, the programme ³_____ (stop) and the presenter said that Elvis ⁴_____ (die) earlier that day. Mum was only a school girl then so she ran downstairs and ⁵_____ (tell) her parents. They ⁶_____ (watch) television and they weren't very interested so my mum phoned her friend. Her friend ⁷_____ (not hear) the news and she ⁸_____ (not believe) my mum until she saw the news that evening. That's because my mum would often ⁹_____ (play) tricks on her friends. She ¹⁰_____ (use to) love thinking of stories to tell them and watching them when they realised they weren't true!

/10

4 used to and would **Complete the table with sentences that mean the same as the Past Simple sentence. Write a cross (X) when you can't make a sentence.**

Past Simple	Used to	Would
I went to the cinema every weekend when I was young.	I used to go to the cinema every weekend when I was young.	I would go to the cinema every weekend when I was young.
I loved cowboy films.	I used to love cowboy films.	X
I didn't have much money then.	1	2
My grandfather gave me the money for the cinema.	3	4
I was very sad when he died.	5	6
He came to dinner with us every Sunday.	7	8

/8

TOTAL SCORE **/30**

Module Diary

1 **Look at the objectives on page 13 in the Students' Book. Choose three and evaluate your learning.**

1 Now I can _____
well / quite well / with problems.

2 Now I can _____
well / quite well / with problems.

3 Now I can _____
well / quite well / with problems.

2 **Look at your results. What language areas in this module do you need to study more?**

Amazing rescue in Chile

One of the most amazing news stories of 2010 came from Chile where thirty-three men had been 700 metres under the ground for 69 days. When they finally came out, there were celebrations not just in the town of Copiapo but all over Chile and, in fact, all over the world. We talked to José, a Chilean man who lives in London.

Did you watch everything, José?

Yes, we did. We stayed awake all night because it was just so *heartwarming*. We had a big party and, every time another man came out, we all hugged each other and cheered. We were *over the moon*. The neighbours came to ask us to be quiet but, when they saw what was happening, they joined in and stayed with us until the morning.

Did you know any of the men?

No, I come from Santiago. Copiapo is 800 kilometres north of Santiago. I've never been there. In fact I didn't know exactly where it was until the accident. I know that one of my friends from university went out with a girl from Copiapo. She was studying in Santiago. He never went to her hometown or met her family, though.

What was your reaction when the last man came out?

We couldn't believe it. We were sure there would be an accident. Right up to the last minute *our hearts were in our mouths*. When we finally knew everything was all right, we laughed a lot and sang Chilean songs. I cooked Cazuela which is a traditional Chilean food made from chicken and different vegetables. Then the phone started to ring. Friends and family from all over the world wanted to know if we had seen the news. No one had phoned while it was happening because no one wanted to miss anything.

What did you do the next day?

At first, I wanted to go back to Chile. I spent some time on the internet looking for plane tickets but they were really expensive so I decided not to buy one. In the end, I realised *it was pointless* and that my life was now here in London. I have a wife and children here and this restaurant. Chile is in my heart but I don't need to be there.

Have you heard about the celebrations in Chile?

Oh, of course. My aunt told me all about them. She went to the main square in the town, the Plaza de Armas, in the morning because she had heard on the radio that some of the men were safe. She didn't leave until the last man had come out which was about 9 p.m. in Chile. She said the atmosphere was amazing.

Reading

❶ **Read the text on the left. Are the sentences are true (T) or false (F)?**

1 The celebrations were not just in Chile. ___
2 José spent the night watching television alone. ___
3 The people hugged each other a lot that night. ___
4 He had never heard of Copiapo before the accident. ___
5 José's friend had been to Copiapo. ___
6 There were no phone calls until the last man was safe. ___
7 José bought a plane ticket but he didn't use it. ___
8 His aunt was in the square from the time the first man came out until the last one came out. ___

❷ **Look at the four expressions in bold from the text. Decide on the best meaning for each one. Use the context of the text to help you.**

1 heartwarming - making you feel *hot/happy/in love*
2 over the moon - *very happy/very tired/very quiet*
3 our hearts were in our mouths - we were *very excited/very tired/very nervous*
4 it was pointless - *it was impossible/there was no reason for it/it was important*

Listening

❸ **🔊1.14** **Listen to a talk about a music festival and choose the best answers.**

1 Liet International is the name of a:
 a band. **b** organisation. **c** festival. **d** song.
2 The winners of the 2009 festival:
 a sang in Finnish. **b** were from Finland. **c** were the first Sami group to win the competition. **d** were all eighteen years old.
3 Miira Suomi is:
 a a place. **b** a song. **c** a group. **d** a person.
4 Nos Ur is a song competition for:
 a English speakers. **b** British bands. **c** bands from the British Isles and an area of France. **d** the winners of the Liet festival.
5 Sunrise Not Secular:
 a are punks. **b** are from Scotland. **c** are girls. **d** were the only winners of the Nos Ur festival.
6 The main difference between Nos Ur and Nos Og is that:
 a the bands in Nos Og are younger. **b** the musical styles in Nos Og are more traditional. **c** Nos Og is open to bands from different places to Nos Ur. **d** there is no competition in Nos Og.

Speaking

❹ **🔊1.15** **Read the conversation between an examiner and two students. Complete the phrases the students use to agree and disagree with each other. Then listen to check.**

Examiner: What do you think of international sports competitions?

A: Well, the biggest are the Olympics but I'm not really interested in them.

B: ¹ *Neither am* I. They're really boring. I love football, though.

A: ²_____ _____ I. Especially the cup final. I'm very excited about the Wimbledon tennis championships this year, too.

B: ³_____ _____ I. I hope the British players do well this time.

Examiner: What environmental problems are you worried about?

A: We have had floods near our house so I'm worried about them.

B: I'm ⁴_____. We don't live near a river so we're safe. We get a lot of pollution from traffic, though.

Examiner: Do you take an interest in the world's problems?

A: No, I'm not interested in disasters in other countries.

B: I ⁵_____. I always try to do something to help.

Examiner: Are you interested in the lives of famous people at all?

A: I sometimes read about them in newspapers and magazines but I never watch funerals or weddings of famous people.

B: ⁶_____ _____ I. I can't understand why anyone is interested.

Examiner: What are your favourite days?

A: I guess my birthday is the most important to me. I always have a big party.

B: I ⁷_____. I never celebrate my birthday but I like other people's.

A: Why don't you celebrate your birthday?

B: I don't want to grow old.

A: I ⁸_____, well, not old but I can't wait until I'm old enough to get a job and start earning some money.

❺ **🔊1.16** **Decide which replies could be replaced with *me too* and which with *me neither*. Then listen to check.**

Exam Choice 1

Use of English

6 **Read about a special day and choose the correct answers below.**

My family roots are ¹_____ Vietnam but I ²_____ in Australia since I was two years old. I love my new country but I still think of myself as Vietnamese. My grandmother ³_____ tell me stories about the country when I was young and I loved hearing them. That's why I like the Moon Lantern Festival so much. It takes place in the autumn and it's a great time for us to meet ⁴_____ with our family and friends who live in different parts of Australia. Before ⁵_____ to the festival, my mum always makes special moon cakes. So ⁶_____ I now, although mine aren't as good as my mum's!

Lots of non-Vietnamese Australians come to the festival. It's very ⁷_____-known and popular. They come to eat the food, listen to the music and watch the dancing. I love Vietnamese dancing and I always join ⁸_____. My dad says that when I dance, I ⁹_____ my mum when she was young.

My favourite time is the evening. We all walk along carrying lights and then there's a big firework display. ¹⁰_____ watching the fireworks, we go to my aunt's house for the night as she lives near the park. The Moon Lantern Festival is my favourite time of the year.

1 a on	**b** at	**c** in
2 a am living	**b** have lived	**c** live
3 a had	**b** used to	**c** has
4 a up	**b** out	**c** off
5 a going	**b** go	**c** went
6 a am	**b** have	**c** do
7 a good	**b** well	**c** famous
8 a in	**b** on	**c** up
9 a like	**b** look	**c** look like
10 a after	**b** while	**c** before

Writing

7 **Complete the answers to the questions with the words below.**

> fashion-conscious
> actors, like Tom Cruise, Johnny Depp and Ewan McGregor
> reading   blonde   slim   easy-going   watching TV
> skiing   sports, like basketball, football and hockey
> hard-working   tall   taking photographs   good-looking
> urban tribes, like goths, punks and emos.

1 What is he like? _____, _____, _____

2 What does she like doing? _____, _____, _____, _____

3 What does she look like? _____, _____, _____, _____

4 Can you give me some examples? _____, _____, _____

8 **Write a description of a friend or member of your family. Include the things below. Write 120 to 150 words.**

- What he/she looks like
- What he/she is like
- What he/she likes doing

TOPIC TALK – VOCABULARY

1 Find ten food words in the text and write them in the correct places in the table.

Cereals	Dairy products	Seafood	Vegetables	Fruit
bread				

People often ask me how I can stay so slim although I don't do much exercise. I am careful about what I eat and when I eat. I always have a big breakfast with two or three slices of bread with butter on them. I also drink coffee and mineral water. At work, I have a yoghurt during the morning and an apple. Sometimes I have a carrot, too. Most people get snacks from the machine but I know they're unhealthy so I never do. For lunch, we often go out and I eat sushi with rice. I love it. It's nice with some lemon to give it a lovely sour flavour. In the evening, I try not to have meat. I usually have fish with some boiled potatoes but not too many and no later than six o'clock.

2 Complete the words in the texts. The number of gaps shows the number of letters in the words.

'I always try to buy ¹o r _g_ _a_ n _i_ c vegetables because they are much healthier than normal ones.'

'This café sells real, ²h _ _ _ -m _ d _ cakes. The owner cooks them in the morning before they open. They are ³d _ l _ c _ _ _ _, but I know they are very ⁴f _ t t _ _ _ n _, especially the ⁵c _ _ _ m _ ones!'

'I can't understand why people buy ⁶f _ _ t food like burgers. It's unhealthy, full of ⁷f _ _, it has lots of ⁸c _ l _ _ _ e _ and, really, it's usually really ⁹d _ _ g _ _ t _ _ _. That's my opinion, anyway.'

'I do a lot of running, so I need to eat a lot of ¹⁰c _ _ b _ h _ _ r _ _ e _. That's why I eat so much pasta.'

3 Complete the dialogue with the phrases below.

all-time favourite meal   bad for you   ~~eat a lot of~~
I'd like to try   I'd never try   it's got a lot of   meal for me
minerals and proteins   tastes delicious

A: What kind of food do you like?

B: Well, I ¹ _eat a lot of_ Chinese and Indian food. I make my own because the food you get in restaurants is very ²_____ because ³_____ fat in it. ⁴_____ some real Chinese food from China to see how different it is. The most important ⁵_____ is breakfast. I always have a grapefruit. My family think I'm crazy but it wakes me up. I also have toast with marmite.

A: What's marmite?

B: It's an English breakfast food. You put it on bread. It ⁶_____ and there are lots of important ⁷_____ in it. However, my ⁸_____ is roast beef. I'll eat most things but ⁹_____ a chip butty. I've seen them on the Internet and they look disgusting.

4 Match the words below with the pictures and label the pictures.

apple   bacon and   chip   chocolate   fish and   ~~roast~~

~~beef~~   butty   cake   chips   eggs   pie

1
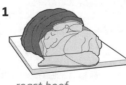
roast beef

2

_____

3

_____

4

_____

5

_____

6

_____

Reading

1 Read the text about seven different celebrity chefs. Match the names (1-7) with the information (a-g).

1 Keith Floyd ___
2 Delia Smith ___
3 Jamie Oliver ___
4 Gordon Ramsay ___
5 Nigella Lawson ___
6 The Hairy Bikers ___
7 Ching He Huang ___

a is popular in America.
b is good-looking.
c has a useful website.
d helps young people.
e lived for a while in South Africa.
f is no longer alive.
g travel a lot.

Celebrity chefs on television

Chefs on television are nothing new but only a few are really worth watching. Here are seven of the best.

(1) _e_ Keith Floyd made a number of successful programmes about cooking. His love for food and people was obvious and he changed TV cookery programmes for ever. Now everyone wants to be like him. Before he started his television career, he had three restaurants which all had financial problems. In fact, even later in life, his restaurants all seemed to lose money. He died in 2009, aged 65.

(2) ___ Delia Smith's 1998 TV series started by showing people how to boil an egg. People love her easy recipes and expert knowledge and she really changes their habits. After her programme about eggs, the number of eggs sold in the UK went up by 10 percent. Her website is useful for people wanting to find out about recipes and places to buy good food.

(3) ___ Jamie Oliver learned to cook as a boy in his parents' pub. As well as cooking, he cares about those less well-off than he is. He gave work to unemployed and homeless young people in his restaurant, Fifteen. His programmes are fun to watch but also show people how to improve their diet, especially a series he made about making school dinners more healthy.

(4) ___ Gordon Ramsay is well-known for his great food and for shouting at people when things go wrong in the kitchen. This has helped him become famous in the USA where his show *Hell's Kitchen* is very popular. He even threw a food reviewer out of his restaurant once because of something the reviewer said.

(5) ___ Nigella Lawson is not a trained chef but her books are very popular. This is because her recipes are simple and she gives advice like a mother or grandmother would, not like an expert. On TV, Nigella is like a friend. Women like her because they want to be like her. Men like her because she is very attractive.

(6) ___ The Hairy Bikers are, as their name suggests, two men with long hair who ride motorbikes. Their show on the BBC is a mixture of cooking and a travel show. They show the people and culture of the places they visit and then some recipes. They have been to lots of different countries and are very passionate about what they do and have a good sense of humour.

(7) ___ Ching He Huang was born in Taiwan but spent most of her childhood in South Africa before coming to England at the age of eleven. Ching's books and TV shows show old meals her grandmother used to cook but she does change them a little so that it is easy for people to find everything needed even in a normal supermarket and to make the recipes as healthy as possible.

2 Read the text again. Match the paragraphs (1-7) with the headings (A-H). There is one extra heading.

- **A** A huge influence
- **B** Famously angry
- **C** Not just cooking
- **D** Liked by all
- **E** Great cook, terrible in business
- **F** Too complicated for most
- **G** Traditional and healthy
- **H** Educating and entertaining

Word Builder Verbs + prepositions

3 Complete the sentences with the correct form of the verbs. There is one extra verb in each box.

be   care   know   ~~talk~~

Today, I'm going to [1]talk_____ to you about healthy food. In my opinion it's important for everyone to [2]_____ about fat, calories, proteins and vitamins and what is and isn't good for us. This is very important in our schools because children often don't [3]_____ about things like that. They are young and healthy and don't realise that what they eat now can cause them problems in the future.

be   care   find out

The new series [4]_____ about traditional food in European countries. You will [5]_____ about the food people eat and also how they lead their lives.

care   know   think

I love food and I spend a lot of time [6]_____ about it. When I was younger, I didn't [7]_____ about food from other countries but now I try something new each week.

Sentence Builder Reason linkers

4 Choose the correct words to complete the sentences. Then decide which of the celebrity chefs in the reading text they are about. Sometimes more than one word is possible.

1 Don't say anything bad about the food *in case*/ *as/because* he throws us out of the restaurant! _Gordon Ramsay_

2 I always loved his programmes *in case/as/because* he made cooking look so fun. _____

3 I love her programme *because/in case/just in case* she's so nice to look at! _____

4 I know eggs are easy to cook but I think we should watch her programme *as/just in case/in case* there's something important we don't know. _____

5 We don't need to go to the Chinese restaurant *because/in case/as* her recipes are so easy to follow. _____

6 He decided to complain about school dinners *in case/because/just in case* no one else seemed to be interested in them. _____

7 They should wear thick clothes *because/as/in case* it's cold while they are riding round. _____

Writing

5 Read the instructions below. Write an invitation in your notebook.

Your family are driving to the seaside on Saturday. You have a place in your car and you want to invite your friend to go with you. Include the details below in your invitation. Use the phrases from the sentence builder.

- Give a reason for going (swimming, sailing, etc.).
- Tell your friend to bring something and give a reason why.
- Tell your friend to contact you (When/How?) and give a reason why.

GRAMMAR
The Passive

REMEMBER

Complete exercises A–B before you start this lesson.

A **Choose the correct words to complete the dialogues.**

1 **A:** *Were you given*/*Did you give* anything nice for your birthday?

   B: Yes, I *gave/was given* lots of things. My uncle *gave/was given* me an MP3 player.

2 **A:** *Has your mum made/Has your mum been made* any biscuits today?

   B: Yes, but there aren't any left. They *have all eaten/have all been eaten*.

3 **A:** *Have you asked/Have you been asked* to the school disco?

   B: Yes. *I've asked/I've been asked* several times but I *haven't said/haven't been said* 'yes' yet.

4 **A:** *Do you tell/Are you told* what time you have to go to bed on summer camp?

   B: Oh yes, it's terrible. We have to go to bed at 10 p.m. The television *switches/is switched* off at 9.30 p.m. and the teachers *check/are checked* the rooms at 10.15 p.m.

B **Complete the sentences with the Present Simple Passive, Past Simple Passive or Present Perfect Passive form of the verbs in brackets.**

1 **A:** What's wrong?

   B: I *haven't been chosen* (not choose) for the school football team.

2 **A:** I found this letter in your school jacket. When _____ (you give) it?

   B: Oh! That. About a week ago. Sorry, I forgot about it.

3 **A:** I love Fridays. No more school for two days.

   B: Yes, but we _____ (always give) extra homework to do.

4 **A:** _____ (you send) an email by Josh last night?

   B: I don't know. I didn't check my emails yesterday. Why? Is it funny?

5 **A:** Do you want to buy these jeans? They're €50.

   B: €50? But they _____ (wear).

1 ***** **Complete the sentences with the words in capitals.**

1 ARE USED / USE

   We only ___*use*___ organic vegetables in our meals.
   Only organic vegetables _____ in our meals.

2 IS OFTEN EATEN / OFTEN EAT

   Bacon _____ for breakfast in England.
   People _____ bacon for breakfast in England.

3 WROTE / WAS WRITTEN

   Jamie Oliver's book _____ after he made the TV series.
   Jamie Oliver _____ his book after he made the TV series.

4 WAS PREPARING / WAS BEING PREPARED

   When we arrived, the cook _____ dinner.
   Dinner _____ when we arrived.

5 ARE BEING BUILT / ARE BUILDING

   Workers _____ two new restaurants in our town.
   Two new restaurants _____ in our town.

6 HAD EATEN / HAD BEEN EATEN

   By the time we arrived, all the food _____.
   By the time we arrived, the other people at the party _____ all the food.

7 ARE GOING TO PUT / ARE GOING TO BE PUT

   I can't believe that these chips _____ into a sandwich.
   I can't believe you _____ these chips into a sandwich.

8 CAN BE MADE / CAN MAKE

   You _____ cakes with butter or margarine.
   Cakes _____ with butter or margarine.

9 WERE CLEANING / WERE BEING CLEANED

   The restaurant tables _____ when we arrived.
   They _____ the restaurant tables when we arrived.

10 COOKED / WAS COOKED

   The special meal _____ last night.
   They _____ the special meal last night.

2 ** Complete the text with the correct Passive form of the verbs in brackets.

Come to Roskilly's Farm for a perfect ice cream

The first Roskilly farm ¹ _was built_ (build) in Cornwall in 1963 and buildings ² _____ (add) since then. It was in 1987, though, that Roskilly's started to become really famous. Ice cream ³ _____ (produce) there three years earlier but it hadn't been a success. However, an expert ice cream maker ⁴ _____ (invite) to the farm in 1987 and he was able to show them what they were doing wrong. After his visit, twenty different flavours of ice cream ⁵ _____ (offer) to the public and that number has steadily grown so that, now, a total of forty flavours can ⁶ _____ (buy). In the future it is likely that even more flavours ⁷ _____ (create) to be enjoyed by Roskilly's customers. Roskilly's ⁸ _____ (visit) by thousands of holiday makers every year. The farm can ⁹ _____ (visit) for free, leaving customers with more money to spend on the delicious, organic products which ¹⁰ _____ (sell) in the cafés and shops there. More attractions ¹¹ _____ (now build) at Roskilly's to make it even more popular in the future.

3 *** Complete the second sentence so that it has the same meaning as the first.

1 I cooked the beef for three hours.
The beef _____ _was cooked for three hours._ _____

2 You should take the egg out of the water after three minutes.
The egg _____

3 They're going to eat dinner at 8 p.m.
Dinner _____

4 The chef is teaching us how to cook duck today.
We _____

5 They will only grill your steak for a few seconds on each side.
Your steak _____

6 They chef hadn't told anyone about his recipe before.
No one _____

7 How long did they fry this chicken for?
How long was _____

8 What do people usually eat with sushi?
What is _____

Grammar Alive Describing a process

4 Complete the sentences with the phrases below.

are now grown   can be kept   can still be found
~~have been grown~~   were brought   were eaten

1 Potatoes _have been grown_ in Peru for thousands of years.

2 Thousands of different types of potatoes _____ there, more than in any other part of the world.

3 One reason for their success there is that they _____ for several years because of the cold mountain nights.

4 Potatoes _____ to Europe by the Spanish in 1536.

5 In 2008, a total of 314 million tonnes of potatoes _____.

6 Surprisingly, 33 percent of all potatoes _____ in China and India.

Listening

1 Complete the names of the courses you can have in a three course meal.

1 _starter_ or _____ course.
2 _____ course.
3 _____

2 Put these events in the order they happen.

a Ask for the menu. ___
b Leave a tip. ___
c Book a table. _1_
d Pay the bill. ___
e Order food. ___

3 Where can you eat? Complete the places. Look at the things people say to help you.

1 'Just a coffee for me, please.'
a c _a_ _f_ _é_ / a c _ _ _ _ _ h _ _ _ _
2 'Burger and chips, please.'
a f _ _ _ - f _ _ _ b _ _
3 'One large cheese and tomato pizza, please.'
a p _ _ _ _ r _ _
4 'We'll get some Chinese and eat it at home while we watch a DVD'   t _ _ _ - a _ _ _
5 'Choose your food and serve yourself.'
s _ _ _ - s _ _ v _ _ _ restaurant.
6 'Let's eat here – it's healthier than having meat.'
a v _ g _ _ _ r _ _ _ restaurant.

Talk Builder Eating out

4 **1.17** Listen to the conversation and complete the bill.

DELICIOUS
r e s t a u r a n t

Starters: ¹v_egetable_ s_____
²p_____ c_____

Main courses: ³c_____
s_____ (no n_____ or h_____)
⁴s_____ (r_____) and c_____

Desserts: ⁵a_____ p_____
with c_____

Drinks: ⁶A b_____ of w_____
(1_____) ⁷c _____
(b_____) ⁸c _____

TOTAL: ⁹£_____
Paid by ¹⁰c_____

5 Complete the dialogue with the phrases below.

I take   ~~table for two~~   we have the menu   we're out of
would you like   we have the bill   you got a reservation
you like to pay   you mind waiting   you ready to order

Waiter: Good evening, sir, madam.
Man: Good evening. A ¹___ _table for two_ ___, please.
Waiter: Have ²_____?
Man: No, we haven't. Is that a problem?
Waiter: No. We'll have a table soon. Would ³_____ for a few minutes?
Man: No, that's fine.
Waiter: Can ⁴_____ your coats?
Man: Thank you.
Waiter: Please sit here while you're waiting.
Man: Could ⁵_____, please? We can look at it while we're waiting.
Waiter: Of course. Here you are.
...
Waiter: The table is free now. Please, come this way.
Man: Thank you.
Waiter: Are ⁶_____?
Man: Yes. We'd like two vegetable soups and two fish and chips.
Waiter: ⁷_____ fish I'm afraid.
Man: Oh, well, a chicken salad for me. What about you?
Woman: I'll have the grilled steak, please.
Waiter: How ⁸_____ the steak?
Woman: Rare, please.
...
Man: Could, ⁹_____, please?
Waiter: Certainly, sir. Would ¹⁰_____ by cash or credit card?
Man: Credit card, please.

6 **1.18** Now listen to the dialogue to check your answers.

Check Your Progress 3

1 Food **Complete the sentences with the words below. There are two extra words.**

calories   dairy   fibre   home-made   organic   seafood   vegetarian

1 My doctor told me not to eat so many _____ products so I've stopped eating cheese, butter and yoghurts.
2 I'm not a _____ but I try not to eat meat more than once a week.
3 We need to eat food that is low in fat and high in _____ if we want to lose weight and be healthy.
4 How many _____ are there in this small piece of cake? 200? 300?
5 I don't eat meat, just fish and other _____.

/5

2 Verbs and prepositions **Choose the correct words to complete the sentences.**

1 Today I am going to *talk/think/learn* to you about vegetarian cookery.
2 At school I *learnt/knew/cared* about modern world history.
3 Did you *find out/know/be* any information about the new restaurant?
4 What *is/thinks/talks* this book about?
5 Do you *know/learn/care* anything about cooking with herbs?

/5

3 Reason linkers **Rewrite the sentences with the same meaning as the one above using the words in capitals.**

1 You might be hungry on the journey so I've made you some sandwiches.
BECAUSE _____
IN CASE _____
2 You might want to contact us so take your mobile phone.
JUST IN CASE _____
BECAUSE _____
3 I want to save some money so I'm going to work all summer.
AS _____
BECAUSE _____

/6

4 The Passive **Complete the dialogues with the correct form of the verbs in capitals.**

ADD ASK GIVE MAKE

A: Waiters have a difficult job and, in the rush to serve everyone, mistakes [1]_____ sometimes _____. Josh is a waiter. Josh, what is the most usual mistake and why does it happen?

B: I think the most common mistake is when something [2]_____ to the bill which the customers didn't eat or drink. Of course, if one person [3]_____ to pay extra, it usually means that someone else [4]_____ something for nothing.

ADD COOK PUT(x 2)

A: We went to a cake factory on a school trip. When we arrived, the chocolate [5]_____ on top of the cakes. They [6]_____ a few hours earlier and had to be cool before the chocolate [7]_____. When the chocolate is hard, the cakes can [8]_____ into boxes.

/8

5 Eating out **Choose the correct words to complete the sentences.**

1 A *seat/table/menu* for two, please.
2 Have you got *a bill/a reservation/an order*?
3 I'm afraid we're *away from/out of/down on* chicken.
4 How would you *have/like/be* your steak?
5 I'll *have/have/take* the chicken, please.
6 *Will/Could/Do* we have the bill, please?

/6

TOTAL SCORE   */30*

Module Diary

1 Look at the objectives on page 21 in the Students' Book. Choose three and evaluate your learning.

1 Now I can _____
well / quite well / with problems.
2 Now I can _____
well / quite well / with problems.
3 Now I can _____
well/ quite well / with problems.

2 Look at your results. What language areas in this module do you need to study more?

Sound Choice 2

Sound Check

Say the words and expressions below.

a We'd been there, I'd never seen (Exercise 1)

b We used to go, We didn't use to go (Exercise 2)

c danced, ordered, tasted (Exercise 3)

d trophy, grilled, chocolate (Exercise 4)

e it/eat, full/fool, wok/walk (Exercise 5)

f wedding, marriage, occasion (Exercise 6)

g I'd just finished my meal. So, the next thing I did was (Exercise 7)

h And then?, Wow!, Amazing (Exercise 8)

i vegetarian, police, dairy (Exercise 9)

1.19 **Listen and check your answers. Which sounds and expressions did you have problems with? Choose three exercises to do below.**

1 **1.20** **Grammar - contractions Listen and repeat the sentences.**

1 We'd been there for three hours.
2 I'd never seen it.
3 He'd forgotten his bag.
4 They'd lost every game.
5 You'd gone home.
6 It'd been a good party.

2 **1.21** **Grammar -** *used to* **Listen to the sentences. Does the speaker say the word** *used* **or** *use* **in each sentence?**

1	_used_	3	_____	5	_____
2	_____	4	_____	6	_____

3 **1.22** **Grammar - regular past endings** /d/, /t/, /ɪd/ **Write the words in the correct column depending on the sound of the final** -ed**. Then listen to check.**

~~ordered~~ celebrated
hugged elected danced reserved
attacked tasted laughed

/d/	/t/	/ɪd/
ordered	_____	_____
_____	_____	_____
_____	_____	_____

4 **1.23** **Consonant clusters at the beginning of a word Write the two consonants at the beginning of each word.**

1	_sp_	5	_____	8	_____
2	_____	6	_____	9	_____
3	_____	7	_____	10	_____
4	_____				

5 **1.24** **Vowels Listen to the words. Number the words in the order you hear them (1 or 2).**

1	it	1	eat	2	5 bit ☐	beat ☐
2	full	2	fool	1	6 pull ☐	pool ☐
3	not	☐	nought	☐	7 at ☐	art ☐
4	wok	☐	walk	☐	8 had ☐	hard ☐

6 **1.25** **Spelling - double consonants Listen to the words. Which letter is doubled?**

1	_wedding_	4	_____	7	_____
2	_____	5	_____	8	_____
3	_____	6	_____	9	_____

7 **1.26** **Expressions - sentence stress** <u>Underline</u> **the word(s) with the main stress. Listen to check your answers and repeat the sentences.**

1 I'd <u>just</u> finished my meal …
2 So, the next thing I did was …
3 Would you mind waiting here …
4 Could we have the menu, please?
5 It was the weirdest thing that has ever happened to me.

8 **1.27** **Expressions Listen and say which reply sounds as if the speaker is interested.**

1 _Reply 2_
2 _____
3 _____
4 _____

9 **1.28** **Difficult words - word stress Listen to the words and match them to the correct stress patterns.**

oO	Oo	Ooo	oOo	oOoo	ooOoo
					anniversary

TOPIC TALK - VOCABULARY

1 Label the types of homes. You can see the first letter of each word.

1
a b*ungalow*_____

2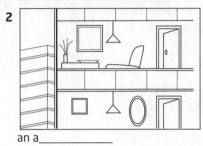
an a_____

3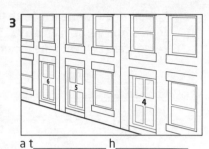
a t_____ h_____

4
a d_____ h_____

5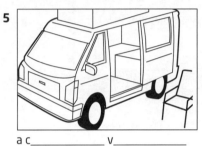
a c_____ v_____

6
a c_____

2 Match questions (1-6) with the answers (a-f).

1 What kind of house do you live in? _d_
2 What appliances has it got in the kitchen? ___
3 How do you keep the house warm? ___
4 Where is the house? ___
5 Why do you like it? ___
6 What is your dream house? ___

a We've got central heating.
b I'd love to live in a cottage in the country.
c It's cosy and quiet.
d A flat.
e In the suburbs.
f An oven, a dishwasher and a fridge/freezer.

3 Complete the text with the words below. There are three extra words.

bedrooms ~~bungalow~~ centre cupboards fireplace fitted heating home machine outskirts space suburbs

I live in a ¹ _bungalow_ . It's got three
² _____, a living room and a big kitchen.
There is lots of ³ _____ in the house and
⁴ _____ wardrobes in all the bedrooms. It's
got central ⁵ _____ for the winter so it's
nice and warm. We've got a washing ⁶ _____
for washing our clothes. It's in the bathroom
downstairs. I love watching films and we've got a
great ⁷ _____ cinema in the living room. The
house is on the ⁸ _____ of a big town. It's
about twenty minutes from the town ⁹ _____
by bus.

4 Find the word that does not fit in each category. Explain why it does not fit.

1 **a** outskirts **b** suburbs **c** views **d** downtown
_____ *views – the rest describe location* _____

2 **a** air-conditioning **b** cosy **c** fireplace **d** terrace
_____

3 **a** bungalow **b** hut **c** apartment **d** lawn
_____

4 **a** village **b** oven **c** fridge **d** dishwasher
_____

5 **a** lawn **b** pond **c** garden **d** freezer
_____

6 **a** quiet **b** flat (n) **c** warm **d** cosy
_____

Present Perfect Continuous

REMEMBER

Complete exercises A-B before you start this lesson.

A Complete the sentences with the Present Perfect form of the verbs in brackets. Then match the sentences (1-4) with the pictures (a-d).

a [2] Why are you under the desk?

b ☐ Are you going to buy it?

c ☐ What's wrong with your watch?

d ☐ Where's your computer?

1 Someone _has taken_ (take) it to use at their house.

2 I _____ (lose) my pen.

3 It _____ (stop).

4 No, I _____ (spend) all my money.

B Use the cues to make questions and short replies in the Present Perfect.

1 A: you / ever / be / to Italy?
  B: ✓
  A: _Have you ever been to Italy?_
  B: _Yes, I have._

2 A: you / ever / eat snake?
  B: ✗
  A: _____
  B: _____

3 A: your mum / ever / wear / a football team shirt?
  B: ✓
  A: _____
  B: _____

4 A: your sister / ever / give / you good advice?
  B: ✗
  A: _____
  B: _____

❶ * Complete the sentences using the Present Perfect Continuous.

1

He / play computer games
He's been playing computer games.

2

She / cut onions _____

3

They / run _____

4

She / clean _____

5

He / cook _____

6

They / swim _____

2 ** Complete the dialogue with the Present Perfect Continuous form of the verbs in brackets.

A: Mum and dad want to sell our house and move so they've been very busy trying to make it look nice.

B: What ¹ _have they been doing_ (they do)?

A: They ² _____ (paint) the house. Mum ³ _____ (also / tidy) the garden and dad ⁴ _____ (clean) the kitchen. They haven't finished yet but it looks much nicer than before.

B: ⁵ _____ (you help) them?

A: No, I haven't. I ⁶ _____ (study). I've got exams next week and I've got lots of work to do. For the last two weeks, I ⁷ _____ (go) to bed at 2 a.m. and I ⁸ _____ (not eat) properly. I'm glad the exams will be over soon.

3 *** Use the cues to complete the dialogues in the Present Perfect Continuous and the Present Perfect.

1 A: What / you / do this morning?

B: I / write / emails

A: How many / you / write?

B: I / write seven so far.

A: _What have you been doing this morning?_

B: _I've been writing emails._

A: _How many have you written?_

B: _I've written seven so far._

2 A: Where are your parents?

B: They're shopping. They / shop all morning. _____

They're buying furniture for the new house.

A: What / they / buy / so far? _____

B: They / buy a sofa and two armchairs. _____

Now, they're looking for a kitchen table.

3 A: You look tired.

B: I am. I / work all morning. _____

A: Really? You / do / housework? _____

B: Yes. I / clean. _____

A: you / finish? _____

B: Nearly. I / clean _____ the kitchen and living room but I / not tidy _____ my bedroom yet.

Grammar Alive Explanations

4 Complete the dialogues with the ideas below in the Present Perfect Continuous and Present Perfect.

> argue   decide not to go out with each other anymore
> not have a chance to change my clothes yet
> not score yet   play for ten minutes
> see it three times - always cries   walk in the rain
> ~~watch a sad film~~

A: Your sister's crying.

B: I know. ¹ _She's been watching a sad film._
² _____

A: Sue and Dave look upset.

B: They are. ³ _____ and I think
⁴ _____

A: They're playing already.

B: Yes. ⁵ _____ but don't worry,
⁶ _____.

A: Your clothes are wet.

B: I know. ⁷ _____
⁸ _____

11

SKILLS
Listening

1 Look at the title and the photo. What do you think are the answers to questions (1–3)?

The eighth wonder of the world can be yours ... for a few days at least.

1 Where do you think it is?
  a Dubai **b** The USA
2 What do you think the title means?
  a You can buy a house there. **b** You can rent a holiday home there.
3 What does the shape of the island look like?
  a An animal **b** A tree

2 **1.29** Listen to a talk about the islands in the photos. Complete the information in the notes.

Palm Island

Work began in ¹_____.

It is the largest ²_____ island in the world.

The bridge to Dubai is ³_____ metres long.

The sand they used to make the islands came from the bottom of the ⁴_____ _____

The island cost ⁵$_____ billion to build.

The World is bigger and slightly ⁶_____ _____ than Palm Island

The houses on Palm Island have got six ⁷_____.

There is a door from the kitchen to the ⁸_____ outside.

There is room for ⁹_____ _____ in the garage.

The cheapest time of year to stay on Palm Island is in the ¹⁰_____ .

Sentence Builder Modifiers and comparatives

3 Look at the information about houses 1 and 2. Choose the correct words to complete the text.

House One:
3 bedrooms
Built: 2008
Price: $400,000
The greenest house ever in 2008.

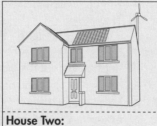

House Two:
4 bedrooms
Built: 2009
Price: $2 million
The new greenest house ever 2009, 2010, 2011.

House One has got three bedrooms. It was built in 2008 and it costs $400,000. In 2008, it was the greenest house in the UK. House Two is ¹*a bit/much bigger* than House One. It has got four bedrooms. House One is ²*slightly/much* older than House Two and House Two is ³*a bit/much* more expensive than House One. House One was the greenest house in the UK in 2008 but House Two is ⁴*slightly/even* greener than House One.

Word Builder Prepositons and adverbs

4 Choose the correct words to complete the text.

From:	Simon
To:	Rosa

Hi,

I'm writing to you all about my party. My parents have agreed that I can have it in the living room. That is ¹*downstairs/ go downstairs*, next to the kitchen. My bedroom is ²*above/ upstairs* the living room and my parents' room is at the back of the house so it won't be so noisy there. We can play our music loud! The living room is quite big. ³*In/On* one side of the room are a big sofa and a coffee table. ⁴*Along/In* the corner there is a TV and ⁵*go along/along* one wall there are shelves with my parents' books and CDs on them. You mustn't touch them.

When you arrive, ⁶*get onto/go along* the path and ⁷*onto/ into* the terrace. The doors to the living room will be open so ⁸ *inside/go inside*. Don't go to the front door. We'll keep the terrace doors open. If you want to dance, ⁹*go outside/ outside*. I don't want anything in the living room broken!

The party will start at 8 p.m. and finish at midnight. See you there.

Simon

LESSON

12

GRAMMAR

have/get something done

1 * **Look at the list. Complete the sentences with the correct form of *to have* and *to get*.**

> ### Jobs for the house
>
> **Every week:**
>
> Grass cut (have)
>
> Windows washed (have)
>
> **Last month:**
>
> Roof repaired (get)
>
> Living room painted (have)
>
> **Next month:**
>
> Washing machine checked (get)
>
> **Done:**
>
> Old cupboards removed (have)
>
> **Not done:**
>
> New cupboards put in. (have)
>
> **Have to do:**
>
> Oven fixed (get)

1 We ___*have*___ our grass cut and our windows washed every week.

2 We _____ our roof repaired last month.

3 We _____ our living room painted last month.

4 We _____ our washing machine checked next month.

5 We _____ our old cupboards removed but we _____ the new cupboards put in yet.

6 We have to _____ our oven fixed.

2 ** **Complete the dialogue with the correct form of the verbs in brackets. Use *get* for answers 5 and 7.**

A: Hi, Larry. How's the new house?

B: It's okay but there's still a lot we need to have done. We [1] _have just had the electricity checked_ (just / electricity / check) but we [2] _____ _____ (not / the old windows / replace) yet.

A: What about upstairs? [3] _____ (you / have / the bedrooms / paint) yet?

B: No. We painted them ourselves. Maria and Andy [4] _____ (one room / paint) last year and it cost them over £1000.

A: I know. My dad says that he [5] _____ (going to / central heating / put in) when he can find someone who will do it for less than £5000.

B: Of course. You've still got real fires. [6] _____ (you / fireplaces / clean) this year?

A: Not yet, no but we will [7] _____ (have to / them / do) soon. They're really dirty.

3 *** **Use the cues to write questions and answers.**

1 how often / you / have / your / hair cut
I / about / once / every two months
How often do you have your hair cut?
I have it cut about once every two months.

2 how often / your mum / have / her teeth / check?
She / them / every six months

_____

_____

3 how often / your dad / get / his car / repair?
he / not / get / it / repair. He does everything himself.

_____

_____

4 how many times / your sister / have / her eyes / test / in her life?
she / not / have / them / test. Her eyes are fine.

_____

_____

5 When / you / next have / your photo / take ?
I don't know. I / probably / have it / take / at the end of the school year.

_____

_____

Workshop 2

Writing

1 Look at these questions and the results. What do you do yourself and what do you have done for you?

How independent are you? What do you do and what do you have done for you?

We asked 100 school students aged fifteen to eighteen and this is what we found.

	What do you do?	What do you have done?
1 Repair bike	86%	15%
2 Install new computer programs	92%	8%
3 Make lunch	48%	52%
4 Cut your hair	0%	100%
5 Paint your bedroom	19%	81%

2 Use the information from Exercise 1 to match the beginnings (1-6) with the correct endings (a-f).

1 Approximately half of the teenagers _c_
2 More than 85 percent of the teenagers ___
3 Only 8 percent of the teenagers ___
4 Less than 20 percent of the teenagers ___
5 None of the teenagers ___
6 100 percent of the teenagers ___

a have new computer programs installed for them.
b have their hair cut by someone else.
c make their own lunch.
d cut their own hair.
e repair their own bikes.
f paint their own bedrooms.

3 Cross out the word or phrase which *cannot* replace the underlined words from Exercise 2.

1 *Around/More than*
2 *A few/The majority/Most*
3 *No more than 8 percent/Less than/A few*
4 *Just under/Only/Not more than*
5 *0%/100%*
6 *All/None*

4 Think of your questions to ask. Work in groups or go around the class. Ask your questions and make notes of the answers.

5 Use the ideas from Exercises 1 to 3 and your results to draw a graph. Write a report in your notebook. Write 120 to 150 words.

Speaking

1 Complete the offers with the words below.

can do if let like shall would

1 ___Can___ I help you tidy your room?
2 _____ you want a hand with the washing up?
3 _____ I make a cake for your birthday?
4 _____ you like me to repair your bike?
5 I'll buy some paint for your bedroom _____ you _____.
6 _____ me cook dinner for you tonight.

2 Match the responses (a-f) with the offers (1-6) from Exercise 1.

a No, it's okay, thanks. My mum's made one already. _3_
b Okay great but I don't like cheese. ___
c It's okay, thanks. We've got a dishwasher. ___
d No, thanks. I'm not sure what colour I want yet. ___
e That's very kind of you. It's in the garage. ___
f Yes, please but it's really messy. ___

3 〔1.30〕 Complete the conversation with the phrases below. Then listen to check.

Can I help you?   Do you want a hand with great   if you like   Let me show you   It's okay, thanks. Shall I phone them   That's kind of you,   We'll manage. Would you like me to

Ted: Hello, are you moving in to number six?
Mr Davies: Yes.
Ted: I'm your new neighbour. My name's Ted. [1] *Can I help you?*
Mr Davies: We're okay, thanks.
Ted: [2] _____ carrying boxes or furniture?
Mr Davies: It's okay, thanks. [3] _____
Ted: [4] _____ make you a cup of tea?
Mr Davies: [5] _____, thanks. I hope the people who are helping us arrive soon.
Ted: [6] _____ for you?
Mr Davies: [7] _____ I've got my mobile. I'll phone them after I've finished my tea.
Ted: I'll make some more [8] _____.
Mr Davies: No, thanks. Time to do some work. It's going to be a busy day. Is there a pizzeria near here?
Ted: Yes. [9] _____ where it is. I've got a map.
Mr Davies: Okay, [10] _____.

Check Your Progress 4

1 Houses **Put the words below in the correct categories.**

bungalow air-conditioning cottage nice views
cosy staircase on the outskirts in the suburbs

Types of houses	Advantages
Features	Location

/8

2 Prepositions and adverbs **Complete the sentences with the correct words. You can see the first letter of each word.**

1 Our bedroom is a_____ the living room.
2 O_____, there is a nice garden.
3 There are some shelves a_____ one wall in the living room.
4 U_____, there are three bedrooms and a bathroom. D_____, there is a living room, a kitchen and a second bathroom.

/5

3 Present Perfect Continuous and Present Perfect **Put the verbs in capitals into the correct form.**

TIDY / FIND
I ¹_____ my room all morning and I
²_____ some amazing things.

WAIT / FORGET
Hi Steve, it's me, Elaine. I ³_____ here for ages. Where are you? ⁴_____ our date?

SIT / NOT EAT
What's wrong with Steve? He ⁵_____ in his room all morning. He ⁶_____ even _____ his dinner.

/6

4 have/get something done **Complete the sentences with the correct form of *have/get something done* using the information below.**

Jobs to do this spring
Clean the house – I can do this
Fix the roof – ✔
Paint the kitchen – in June
Replace the fridge – ✔ last week
Mend the sofa – ✔ (John organised it!!)

1 I don't _____ I can clean it.
2 We _____.
3 We _____ in June. It will be easier to organise then.
4 We _____ last week.
5 John _____ so I don't have to worry about this.

/5

5 Offers **Match the beginnings (1-6) with the correct endings (a-f).**

1 Can I ___	a hand with those bags?
2 Do you want a ___	b if you like.
3 Shall I give ___	c help you?
4 Would you like ___	d me to help you?
5 I'll walk home with you, ___	e help you.
6 Let me ___	f you a hand with those bags?

/6

TOTAL SCORE /30

Module Diary

1 **Look at the objectives on page 29 in the Students' Book. Choose three and evaluate your learning.**

1 Now I can _____
well / quite well / with problems.
2 Now I can _____
well / quite well / with problems.
3 Now I can _____
well / quite well / with problems.

2 **Look at your results. What language areas in this module do you need to study more?**

Exam Choice 2

Reading

1 Read the text quickly and answer the question.

Is the text describing:

a a meal?

b a restaurant?

c the food of one country?

Pasties

What are they?

You can find pasties all over Britain and in other countries as well but 'real' pasties are from Cornwall in the south-west of England. The outside, called pastry, is hard and crispy. What goes inside? There are many different answers to that question as we shall see.

A little history

No one knows exactly when pasties first appeared but a note from the King of England that he wrote over 800 years ago says that he wanted 'one hundred fish cooked in twenty-four pasties' every year. We do know why they became popular. For many centuries, men in Cornwall worked underground. It was hard, dirty work and they couldn't go home during the day for lunch. A pasty made with thick pastry stays warm for a long time so they could have a hot lunch at work. They held a small piece in their hands and ate the rest without getting it dirty. They then threw the small, dirty piece away.

So what's inside?

The traditional Cornish Pasty is made from food from the local area. Beef from Cornish cows and vegetables such as potatoes, onions, carrots are used in the pasty. As most people who ate them were poor, there wasn't much meat. You can still buy pasties like this and they are delicious but lots of people now prefer something more interesting or unusual. That's why there are now shops where you can buy lots of different kinds of pasties. Vegetarian, chicken, Chinese style ... In fact, anything you want.

Are they easy to cook?

Yes. You cook the meat and vegetables first, then you make the pastry. You cover the meat and vegetables with the pastry and put it in the oven until it is hard and crispy. If it isn't hard enough, it will break into several small pieces. This is a problem because most people eat them outside using their hands. If the pastry is too hard, though, the pasty isn't as nice.

Is there anything similar anywhere else?

Many countries have similar food. In Poland, pierogi are usually cooked in water and soft but you sometimes find restaurants where they cook them in the oven. They are much smaller and you have six of them rather than one, large pasty. In Spain and Spanish speaking countries in South and Central America, empanadas are very popular and very similar and, from Greece to India, people eat samosas, although these are usually fried not cooked in the oven.

2 Read the text again and complete the information.

1 The food is from _____.
2 People have eaten this food for at least _____.
3 When the workers ate their pasties at lunchtime, they were still _____.
4 The traditional ingredients were all from the _____.
5 Shops now sell lots of different _____.
6 It's important that the pastry is quite hard so that it doesn't _____.
7 People usually use _____ to eat pasties.
8 The main differences between pasties and pierogi are that pierogi are softer and _____.
9 Empanadas are popular in countries where people speak _____.

Listening

3 **1.31** Listen to a talk about environmentally friendly homes. Make notes about the headings below in your notebook.

Where the homes are:

Information about the builder:

History of the builder's company:

What he uses:

Problems:

4 Use your notes from Exercise 3 to answer the questions.

1 Where the homes are:
  a How far from Houston is Huntsville?
  b What is the population of the town?
2 The builder:
  a How do you spell his surname?
  b Name two jobs he had before he started his company.
3 History of the builder's company:
  a What is the name of his company?
  b When did he start his company?
  c How long did it take to build houses at first?
4 What he uses:
  a How much of what he uses to build houses is recycled?
  b When did the local government set up a special area for recycled waste?
5 Problems:
  a How many of the people who bought his houses have now left them?

Speaking

5 **1.32** Look at this role-play between two students in an exam. They have made six mistakes. Find the incorrect words in the text and replace them with the words below. Then listen to check.

hand   can   if   let   like   shall

1 **A:** Good evening. Would I help you?
2 **B:** Yes, please. We need a room for the night. Have you got one?
3 **A:** Wait a minute … Yes, we have. It's on the tenth floor.
4 **B:** That's fine.
5 **A:** There isn't a lift. Do you want a help with your bags?
6 **B:** Yes, please. They're very heavy.
7 **A:** No problem. Would you want someone to show you around the hotel before you go to your room?
8 **B:** Yes, okay. That's a good idea.
9 **A:** I can give you a map of the town too that you like. It shows all the restaurants and shops near here.
10 **B:** Great, thanks. Er, would I give you my passport now?
11 **A:** No, don't worry. I can look at it later. First, make me show you the dining room. It's open now if you're hungry.
12 **B:** Great. We're starving.

Exam Choice 2

Use of English

6 Complete the second sentence with one or two words so that it has the same meaning as the first.

1 My friend sent me a great recipe for chicken curry.
I _____ a great recipe for chicken curry by my friend.

2 Make lots of dinner because Mark's friends might come.
Make lots of dinner in _____ Mark's friend's come.

3 What are you discussing?
What are you talking _____ ?

4 Our new house is slightly smaller than our old one.
Our old house was a _____ bigger than our new one.

5 My parents got someone to put central heating in our new house.
My parents _____ central heating put in our new house.

6 Can I help you?
Would you _____ to help you?

7 Fewer than 10 percent of my friends are vegetarians.
Not _____ than 10 percent of my friends are vegetarians.

8 Someone's going to build a pond in our garden.
We're going _____ a pond built in our garden.

9 They're cooking the bread at the moment.
The bread _____ cooked at the moment.

10 Do you need some help or are you okay?
Do you want a _____ or are you okay?

Writing

7 You are going to have a party. Use your imagination and the ideas below to answer the questions.

1 Why are you having the party?
It's your birthday. / You are moving house and want to say 'goodbye' / Your own idea

2 What should your friend bring and why?
CDs - might want to dance / Pyjamas - might want to stay the night / Your own idea

3 Suggest something your friend should do and why:
Tell you his/her mobile phone number - you might need to get in touch with him/her / Bring some money - you might decide to go out somewhere / Your own idea

8 Your friend can't come to your party. Use your imagination and the ideas below to answer the question.

What is he/she doing? Going away for the weekend / Mum's birthday / Your own idea.

9 Complete the sentences with the correct linking words.

1 I'm having a party b_____ I want to celebrate the end of my exams.

2 Bring a coat i_____ c_____ it rains.

3 Leave home early j_____ i_____ c_____ the bus is late.

4 I'm afraid I can't come to your party a_____ I have to look after my younger brother.

10 Write an invitation to a party using the ideas from Exercises 7 and 9. Then write a reply from a friend saying they can't come. Write between 80 and 100 words for the invitation and 30 to 50 words for the reply.

TOPIC TALK - VOCABULARY

1 Look at the clues and complete the crossword.

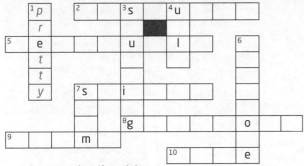

1 attractive (female)
2 strong with large muscles
3 extremely attractive or beautiful
4 very unattractive and unpleasant to look at
5 someone who has a big, strong, body
6 good-looking (male)
7 unattractively thin, too thin / attractively thin
8 extremely attractive or beautiful
9 slightly fat
10 pretty and attractive

2 Complete the gaps with the words below.

big   casual   dinner   low   ~~square~~   wavy

Face
round /
¹ *square* /
long

Forehead
high /
² _____

Chin
³ _____ /
small

Hair
curly /
straight /
⁴ _____

Clothes
⁵ _____ / elegant /
old-fashioned clothes,
leather jackets /
⁶ _____ jackets

3 Cross out the word which is wrong.

1 Jenny is very *attractive/~~long~~/slim*.
2 Kevin is a bit *overweight/high/short*.
3 Tom has got a *long/thin/low face*.
4 Mark has got very big *eyebrows/ears/hair*.
5 Maria is in her *mid/young/late* twenties.
6 Anna wears *wavy/designer/formal* clothes.
7 Natalie wears *long/evening/dinner* dresses.

4 Complete the text with the correct words. You can see the first letter of each word.

The ¹b *est* ____-looking person I know is my boyfriend from school. He's in his ²m_____ teens. He's very ³h_____. In fact, he's ⁴g _____. He's ⁵w_____ b_____ and ⁶m_____ because he goes to the gym a lot. He's got ⁷l_____, ⁸w_____ brown hair, big brown eyes and a big ⁹c_____ (but not too big). He ¹⁰t_____ to wear imaginative clothes, ¹¹l_____ ¹²o_____-f_____ dinner jackets with T-shirts and jeans.

Where do you shop for clothes and why?

We asked our readers for their ideas.

Here are the best two answers.

Anna, Lincoln

My favourite place to buy clothes is in the market. There are lots of different things to buy. Not just clothes but other bits and pieces like jewellery, candles, CDs and other things. The people buying and selling things really want to be there. ¹_c_ Often in shops, the shop assistants are bored or uninterested in the things they are selling. You can find anything in a good market. The clothes are always different and interesting. They are also cheaper than most shops.

One day, I'd like to go to Camden Market in London. It's actually several markets all close to each other. I've read that it gets more visitors than almost any other tourist attraction in London. I think there are only three more popular places. People from all over the world shop there, even the rich and famous. ²___ In most shopping centres, all you can buy is fast food but in markets you can get interesting vegetarian food or food from different countries.

The most important thing, though, are the clothes. Some people like to wear the latest fashions so they go to shops which all sell the same things. ³___ They are the sort of people that shop at markets. In my opinion, they look much more interesting and much better than those who 'follow the crowd.'

Beth, Swansea

I always buy my clothes from the shopping centre. There are lots of different shops there and you can usually find some special offers so the clothes don't have to be expensive. They also have the latest fashions and the right colours. It's important to look right. I don't want anyone laughing at me because of my clothes. The clothes are also good quality and you know that, if there's a problem, we can take the clothes back. The shop will still be there the next week. People in the market might not be.

There are other reasons for shopping there. ⁴___ It doesn't matter if it's raining, snowing or very hot outside. The shopping centre is always dry and warm – not like the market. The shop assistants are usually friendly and helpful. They help you choose the right styles and colours for you but they don't make you buy things that you're not sure about. You can take your time. The other thing I like about the shopping centre is that it isn't just a place to shop. ⁵___ You can eat and drink at one of the restaurants or just sit and watch the people coming and going. Getting there is also nice and easy. There are buses that stop outside the front door and a big, free car park.

❶ Read the texts on the left quickly. Which of these sentences (1-8) are about markets (M) and which are about shopping centres (SC)?

1 All the shops sell the same things. _SC_
2 It's easy to get there. ___
3 The clothes are good quality. ___
4 You can find food from different countries. ___
5 They are usually cheaper. ___
6 It is always dry and warm. ___
7 The people working there really want to be there. ___
8 One is a popular tourist attraction. ___

❷ Read the texts again. Match the sentences (a-f) with the gaps (1-5) in the text. There is one extra sentence.

a It also has great places to eat.
b You can spend the whole day there.
c They are friendly and helpful.
d However, there's nowhere to try clothes on.
e It is always the same temperature.
f Others like to be different and make their own style.

Word Builder Word pairs

❸ Complete the sentences with the words below. There are three extra words.

answer bad dad easy famous friends go paste
pieces slim ~~white~~

1 I love black and _white_ photographs.
2 There are good and _____ things about markets.
3 The restaurant is often full of the rich and _____.
4 I like to spend my free time with family and _____.
5 There will be a chance later to ask and _____ questions.
6 Did you do this homework yourself or did you just cut and _____ it from the internet?
7 The clothes shops here are fine if you are tall and _____, but there's nothing for short, plump people.
8 For my birthday, I got a leather jacket from mum and _____.

Sentence Builder Verb patterns

❹ Use the correct verb pattern for the verbs in brackets. Use _to_ + infinitive, or the infinitive without _to_.

1 Do these shoes make my feet _look_ (look) big?
2 The shop assistants here help you _____ (choose) the right clothes.
3 My parents would like me _____ (wear) smarter clothes.
4 Do you want me _____ (buy) you anything from the shops?
5 Would you like me _____ (make) you a sweater for Christmas?
6 My parents don't want me _____ (get) a tattoo.
7 That leather jacket makes you _____ (look) like a rock star.
8 Can you help me _____ (decide) which shirt to buy?

Writing

❺ Read the instructions below. Write the note and then write a response. Use the phrases in your notes.

- You want to buy some clothes from the internet. Write a note to your older sister asking him/her to help you and to allow you to use their credit card. _Could you help me … ?_

- Respond saying that you are sorry but you can't allow your younger brother/sister to use your credit card. Suggest he/she asks your parents. _I can't …, You should …, Would you like me …, ?_

REMEMBER

Complete exercises A–C before you start this lesson.

A Complete the dialogues with the correct form of *can* or *could*.

A: I had a great time in France in the summer.

B: Really? [1] __*Can*__ you speak French?

A: Yes, I can. I [2]_____ speak French when I was five. I lived in France for three years.

B: Wow, that's great. I [3]_____ speak any languages.

A: Let's go swimming.

B: I [4]_____ swim. I went to lessons but I [5]_____ do it so I stopped going.

A: Really? Come on, I'll teach you.

B: [6]_____ you teach me how to swim?

A: Yes, I think so.

B Complete the sentences with the words below.

> may   must   mustn't

1 You __*mustn't*__ wear that shirt. It's dirty.

2 _____ I leave the lesson early, please?

3 John _____ try to write more carefully.

4 _____ I borrow this CD for a few minutes?

5 You _____ talk during an exam.

6 You _____ remember your mobile phone.

C Which sentences from Exercise B could be written with *can* or *can't*? Write a cross (*x*) when the sentences can't be rewritten.

1 ____*can't*____
2 _____
3 _____
4 _____
5 _____
6 _____

① * Choose the correct word to complete the sentences.

1 I'm sure he's a businessman.
He (must)/might be a businessman.

2 Perhaps she's shopping.
She *must/may* be shopping.

3 It's obvious that she doesn't worry about following fashion.
She *can't/must* worry about following fashion.

4 I'm not sure if Tom is coming with us.
Tom *might not/can't* be coming with us.

5 I'm sure Peter doesn't spend much on his clothes.
Peter *mustn't/can't* spend much on his clothes.

6 It's possible that Top Fashion has got some new clothes today.
Top Fashion *could/must* have some new clothes today.

② ** Match the comments (a–c) to the situations (1–3).

1 a The shopping centre must be closed. _2_
  b The shopping centre could be closed. ___
  c The shopping centre can't be closed. ___

  1 It opens twenty-four hours a day, seven days a week.
  2 There are no cars in the car park.
  3 There was a fire there last week but I'm not sure how bad it was.

2 a That man must be a model. ___
  b That man may be a model. ___
  c That man can't be a model. ___

  1 He's quite good-looking.
  2 He's too short and plump.
  3 People are taking photos of him in different suits.

3 a Debbie must be buying that jacket. ___
  b Debbie might be buying that jacket. ___
  c Debbie can't be buying that jacket. ___

  1 She's giving the shop assistant some money.
  2 It's awful.
  3 I know she likes it.

4 a Maria's T-shirt must be from the market. ___
  b Maria's T-shirt may be from the market. ___
  c Maria's T-shirt can't be from the market. ___

  1 I know she sometimes goes there.
  2 She never shops there.
  3 I've never seen anything like that in the shops.

3 *** **Complete the dialogues with the correct modal *must*, *may*, *might*, *could* or *can't* and the verbs in capitals.**

1 A: Paul's been in the shop a long time. Where is he?

B: There he is. He [1]*must be buying* (BUY) something. He's queuing up at the checkout.

A: He's got a skirt. It [2]_____ (BE) for him! It [3]_____ (BE) a present.

B: You're right. Hey, it [4]_____ (BE) for me!

2 A: What's wrong?

B: I can't find the receipt for these trousers. I want to change them.

A: It [5]_____ (BE) here somewhere. Look in he bag again. You [6]_____ (FIND) it in there.

3 A: I need a new T-shirt.

B: Let's go to 'Cool Fashions'. They [7]_____ (HAVE) something you like.

A: You [8]_____ (THINK) I'm rich. Cool Fashions is the most expensive shop in town.

4 A: Is Sam coming?

B: No.

A: Why not?

B: I'm not sure. He [9]_____ (DO) his homework or he [10]_____ (LOOK) after his young sister.

A: He [11]_____ (LOOK) after his young sister. She's on a school trip this week.

Grammar Alive Gossiping

4 **Look at the pictures and complete the conversations.**

A: She / rich [1]*She must be rich.*

B: Yes and / love shopping [2]_____

A: She / American [3]_____ _____

B: Why do you think that?

A: She looks like Alicia Silverstone in the film *Clueless*.

A: Who are they?

B: They're the same age. They / brother and sister. [4]_____

A: They / brother and sister. They don't look the same [5]_____

B: Not all brothers and sisters look the same. You / know / that [6]_____

A: What do you mean?

B: You and your brother are completely different.

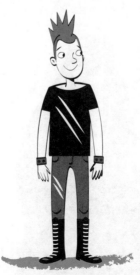

A: What youth tribe do you think he's in?

B: He / an Emo. [7]_____ _____

A: He / an Emo. Emo's don't have spiky hair. [8]_____ _____

B: So what is he?

A: He / a punk with that hair and those clothes. [9]_____ _____

B: He / have a lot of money. [10]_____

A: Why?

B: Those boots are very expensive. I've seen them in the market.

15 SKILLS Listening

1 **Match the words (1–9) with the descriptions (a–i).**

1 Journalists ... _g_
2 The paparazzi ... ___
3 Celebrity gossip magazines ... ___
4 TV talk shows ... ___
5 Stalkers ... ___
6 Websites ... ___
7 Superstars ... ___
8 Positive role models ... ___
9 Negative role models ... ___

a behave badly and have problems with things like drink or the police
b follow their favourite stars wherever they go and become obsessive about them.
c behave well and lead healthy lifestyles.
d can have articles, photos, films, blogs and other things on them.
e are famous all over the world.
f invite stars on to talk about their lives.
g write articles for newspapers and magazines.
h publish photos and articles about stars' private lives.
i take photos of famous people.

Talk Builder Complaining and apologising

2 **1.33 Complete the dialogues with the words below. Then listen to the conversations to check.**

complaint refunds problem never receipt (x 2) refund ~~complain~~ lost make afraid guarantee

1 Customer: I'd like to ¹___complain___ about these trousers.
Shop assistant: Oh yes. What's the ²_____ exactly?
Customer: They've got a hole in them.
Shop assistant: Have you got the ³_____?
Customer: No, I haven't. I ⁴_____ it.
Shop assistant: I'm sorry. I'm ⁵_____ we can't give ⁶_____ without a ⁷_____.
Customer: Oh, right.

2 Customer: I'd like to ⁸_____ a ⁹_____ about this CD player.
Shop assistant: Oh yes. What's wrong with it?
Customer: It doesn't work.
Shop assistant: Let me have a look ... Have you got the ¹⁰_____?
Customer: Yes, here you are.
Shop assistant: Thank you. I'm very sorry about this.
Customer: ¹¹_____ mind.
Shop assistant: Do you want a new one?
Customer: No, thanks. Can I have a ¹²_____, please?
Shop assistant: Yes, of course.

Check Your Progress 5

1 Appearances **Complete the dialogue with the words below. There are three extra words.**

> big   bit   curly   eyes   forehead   gorgeous   jacket   handsome   round   square   stunning   well-built

A: Here are the photos of some possible people for your new advertising campaign. The first one is Henry.

B: He's very ¹_____ but he's a ²_____ old.

A: The next one is Tom.

B: He's got nice, blue ³_____ and lovely ⁴_____ lips but his ⁵_____ is too low.

A: And here is Simon.

B: He's great. He's ⁶_____ and muscular but his hair is too ⁷_____. Who's the last one?

A: This is Lisa.

B: She's ⁸_____. Absolutely ⁹_____.

/9

2 Word pairs **Complete the sentences with the correct words.**

1 Do men and w_____ really use the same changing rooms in some countries?

2 You can b_____ and sell on the internet.

3 Do you ever watch black and w_____ films?

4 Our maths test was nice and e_____.

5 Would you like to be rich and f_____?

/5

3 Modals for speculating **Write sentences using the correct modal *must, could/might/may, might/may not* or *can't*.**

A: The class are really quiet.

B: (It's possible that they're having a test.) They ¹_____.

A: Alex's mum looks about twenty-five.

B: (It's impossible for her to be twenty-five – he's sixteen.) She ²_____.

A: Jenny's got lots of posters of Johnny Depp.

B: (I'm sure she likes him.) She ³_____.

A: Steve's got blond hair but black eyebrows.

B: (It's possible that he isn't really blond.) He ⁴_____.

A: John isn't at school yet and it's 9.15 a.m.

B: (I'm sure he is ill – he's never late for school.) He ⁵_____.

A: No one's answering the door. (It's not possible that they're out.) I can hear voices. They ⁶_____

B: (It's possible that they don't want to see us.) They ⁷_____.

/7

4 Complaining and apologising **Put the dialogue in the correct order.**

Shop assistant: Can I help you?

a I washed it yesterday and it's shrunk. ___

b Yes, here you are. ___

c Yes, I did. I washed it in cold water by hand. ___

d Yes. I'd like to complain about this sweater. ___

e So, not in the machine. Good. Have you got the receipt? ___

f I'd like a refund, please. ___

g What's the problem, exactly? ___

h Oh yes, it has. Did you follow the instructions? ___

i Thank you. We can give you a full refund or a new sweater. ___

Shop assistant: Right. It'll take a few minutes. The manager has to do it.

/9

TOTAL SCORE   */30*

Module Diary

1 Look at the objectives on page 37 in the Students' Book. Choose three and evaluate your learning.

1 Now I can _____.
   well / quite well / with problems.

2 Now I can _____
   well / quite well / with problems.

3 Now I can _____
   well / quite well / with problems.

2 Look at your results. What language areas in this module do you need to study more?

Sound Choice 3

Sound Check

Say the words and expressions below.

a We had our roof fixed. My friend has lost his mobile phone. (Exercise 1)

b My dad was stopped on the way home. Big Ben is visited by thousands of people each year. (Exercises 2 and 3)

c home, brown (Exercise 4)

d trainers, near, boat, because (Exercise 5)

e Can I help you?, Do you want a hand? I'd like a refund. (Exercise 6)

f dung, drink, built (Exercise 7)

1.34 **Listen and check your answers. Which sounds and expressions did you have problems with? Choose three exercises to do below.**

1 **1.35** Grammar – stressed and unstressed *have* **Listen to the sentences and repeat them.**

1 We had our roof fixed.
2 My friend has lost his mobile phone.
3 Dad has his car washed every month.
4 Those paparazzi have been here for ages.
5 Have you finished your dinner?
6 How often do you have your eyes tested?

2 **1.35** Grammar – stressed and unstressed *have* **Listen again and decide whether the vowel sound in the words *have/has/had* is pronounced /æ/ (1) or /ə/ (2).**

a _1_   **c** ___   **e** ___
b ___   **d** ___   **f** ___

3 **1.36** Grammar – unstressed *be* in passives **Listen to the passive verbs and repeat them.**

1 was stopped   4 I've been sent
2 were you given   5 is visited
3 are usually eaten 6 was given

4 **1.37** Grammar – unstressed *be* in passives **Listen to the complete sentences and write the passive verb.**

1 _is visited_   4 _____
2 _____   5 _____
3 _____   6 _____

5 **1.38** Vowels – dipthongs **Listen to the words and underline the word which has a different vowel sound to the others.**

1 home, sew, <u>house</u>
2 own, round, show
3 brown, clothes, around
4 sound, logo, cosy
5 how, found, phone

6 **1.39** Spelling **Listen to the words and write them in the correct column.**

ai	ea	oa
tr**ai**ners	n**ea**r	b**oa**t
_____	_____	_____

7 **1.40** Expressions – sentence stress **Underline the word(s) with the main stress. Then listen to check your answers and repeat the sentences.**

1 Can I <u>help</u> you?
2 Do you want a hand?
3 Shall I carry that for you?
4 Let me show you where it is.
5 Would you like me to help you?
6 I'd like to complain about this skirt.
7 I want to make a complaint.
8 I'd like a refund.

8 **1.41** Difficult words – consonant clusters at the end of a word **Listen to the words and write down the two consonants that come at the end. Listen again and repeat the words.**

1 _ng_   5 _____   9 _____
2 _____   6 _____   10 _____
3 _____   7 _____   11 _____
4 _____   8 _____   12 _____

6 HEROES

TOPIC TALK – VOCABULARY

1 **What are these people campaigning for and against?**

Campaign for

1 'All people are the same.'
e*qual* r*ights*

2 'We can say what we want.'
f_____ of s_____

3 'Men aren't better than us!'
w_____ r_____

4 'Our country must be free.'
i_____

5 'No more war!'
p_____

Campaign against

6 'People younger than sixteen shouldn't have to work.'
c_____ l_____

7 'All people should be free.'
s_____

8 'All people are the same whatever their colour or nationality.'
r_____

9 'All people are the same whatever their nationality, age, sex or religion.'
d_____

10 'Everyone should have enough money to live.'
p_____

2 **Complete the sentences with *joined, studied, took part in* or *worked as a*.**

1 He *studied* law.
2 She _____ lawyer.
3 They _____ a rebellion.
4 We _____ the army.
5 She _____ several protest marches.
6 I _____ the civil service.
7 They _____ medicine.
8 He _____ science.
9 She _____ a scientist.

3 **Complete the sentences with the words below.**

artist explorers leader liberator pioneer
social reformer soldier ~~thinker~~

1 She was a great _thinker_. She read a lot and wrote several books of her ideas.
2 He was a famous _____. He painted people and places.
3 He was one of the first _____. He sailed around the world and discovered several new countries.
4 He was a great _____. He fought in three wars and became a general.
5 She was a strong _____ of her people. They did whatever she said and followed her everywhere.
6 He was the _____ of his country. He organised the rebellion which forced the invaders to leave.
7 She was an important _____. She gave the poor free education and medicine.
8 He was an early _____. He was one of the first people to fly across the Atlantic.

4 **Complete the text about Rosa Parks with the correct words.**

Rosa Parks died in 2005 aged 92. She [1] _was_ a great woman. She [2] _____ from a small town in Alabama in the USA. She was [3] _____ into a poor family and she [4] _____ a difficult childhood. She was small and often ill.

[5] _____ a teenager, she had to leave school to look after her grandmother. After [6] _____, she got married and moved to the town of Montgomery, also in Alabama.

She became famous in 1955. She was on a bus in a seat for black people only. When all the 'white' seats filled up, the driver told her to stand up and let a white person sit down. She refused and was arrested. She spent her life fighting [7] _____ equal rights and [8] _____ racism.

[9] _____ my opinion, she was one of the most important people in the USA in the twentieth century.

GRAMMAR
Speculating about the past

REMEMBER

Complete exercises A-B before you start lesson 18, page 51.

A Look at the information and complete the questions.

Top Fashion

We sell:
T-shirts
Dresses
Skirts
Shirts

Market

We sell:
T-shirts
Jeans
Hats

Melanie went shopping yesterday. She went to Top Fashion. She bought a dress and two T-shirts. She spent €56.00. Charlie went to the market. He bought a pair of jeans and a hat. He spent €20.00.

1 Which __*place sells*__ (place / sell) dresses?
   Top Fashion.
2 What _____ (Top Fashion sell)?
   T-shirts,dresses, skirts and shirts.
3 What _____ (Charlie / buy)?
   A pair of jeans and a hat.
4 _____ (Melanie / buy) a skirt?
   No, she didn't.
5 Who _____ (buy) a hat?
   Charlie.
6 How much _____ (Melanie spend)?
   €56.00.

B Complete the questions with the tags below. There are three extra question tags.

~~aren't there~~   aren't they   are you   do you
don't you   does he   doesn't he
isn't he   is there

1 There are some good shops here, __*aren't there*__ ?
2 You don't like that shirt, _____?
3 Your dad wears some great T-shirts, _____?
4 You go to the market a lot, _____?
5 Prices here are quite low, _____?
6 There isn't much choice here, _____?

1 * Complete the sentences with the correct form of the words in capitals.

'Look, there's a superhero on the roof.'

1 He *must have jumped* up there. MUST / JUMP
2 Or he _____. COULD / FLY
3 Or he _____ up the stairs. MAY / WALK
4 He _____ there long. No one else has seen him yet. CAN'T / BE

'How did she get across?'

5 She _____. It's too far. CAN'T / JUMP
6 And she _____ because she's still dry. CAN'T / SWIM
7 She _____ a boat. COULD / USE
8 She _____ it because I can't see one anywhere. MUST / HIDE

2 ** Complete the dialogues with the correct form of the modals below.

~~can't / be~~ could / switch   might not / be   might / throw
~~must / be~~   must / leave   must / miss

A: Oh no. A traffic jam. There ¹*must have been* an accident.

B: It ²_____ an accident. I was once on a motorway and a lorry was on fire.

A: How did that happen?

B: I don't know. Someone ³_____ a cigarette from a bridge. It ⁴_____ a very big fire because the lorry was okay when we finally passed it but the road was closed for ages.

A: Where's Dan? He's late.

B: He ⁵_____ his bus. Why don't you phone him?

A: I tried but there's no answer. He ⁶_____ it at home.

B: Or he ⁷_____ it off. You know Dan. He switches it off in school and then forgets to switch it on again.

3 *** Read the text and complete the sentences with *must*, *could* and *can't* plus a verb in the correct form.

EMILY DAVISON

She's a hero to many people, especially women. Why? **I'm sure she did** something really special but what? She ¹ *must have done* something really special.

Did she fight for equal rights or **maybe she tried** to start a rebellion? She ²_____ for equal rights for women or she ³_____ to start a rebellion?

She died when a horse hit her. **I'm sure it was** an accident. It ⁴_____ an accident. **Perhaps it was** a police horse. It ⁵_____ a police horse.

It happened at a horse race. She had a return train ticket in her pocket so **I'm sure she didn't want** to die. She ⁶_____ to die. **I'm sure she planned** to go home on the train. She ⁷_____ to go home on the train.

After her death, women's rights in Britain got worse for a few years. Now, she is famous and there is a road named after her.

At the time, **I'm sure that people didn't like** what she did but later, **I'm sure that people's opinions changed**. People ⁸_____ against what she did at the time. Since then, opinions about her ⁹_____.

Grammar Alive Making guesses

4 Look at the pictures and complete the guesses.

1 may / have / bad news?
   He may have had some bad news.

2 could / lose / something
   _____

3 might / hurt / himself
   _____

4 they / must / sell / all the tickets
   _____

5 people / must / get / here early to buy them
   _____

6 someone / might / buy / lots of them to sell them on the internet
   _____

7 it / might / run / away from home
   _____

8 the owner / could / throw / it out of the house
   _____

9 it / might / get / lost while on a walk
   _____

1 **1.42** **Listen to two people talking and choose the best answer to the questions.**

1 What does Alan know about Amelia Earhart?

  a He's never heard of her.

  b He only knows the main event in her life.

  c He's read a lot about her.

2 What didn't Amelia do when she was a child?

  a climb trees

  b go to school

  c try to fly off a roof.

3 Why did she volunteer to work in a hospital?

  a Because she saw injured soldiers coming home from the war.

  b Because she wanted to study medicine.

  c Because she wanted to show that women could do men's jobs.

4 What does Alan think of Sarah's reading?

  a She reads very quickly.

  b She doesn't read carefully.

  c She doesn't read enough.

5 What do they have a different opinion about?

  a Amelia Earhart

  b women's rights

  c computer games

6 What does Sarah like about Amelia Earhart?

  a She was a good flyer.

  b She didn't let problems stop her from doing what she wanted to do.

  c She wore cool clothes.

7 Which sentence about Sarah is true?

  a She never goes out.

  b She tries not to spend anything when she goes out.

  c She doesn't eat anything at the cinema.

8 Which of these is Sarah going to do next year?

  a stay by the sea

  b cycle round England

  c go on holiday with a friend.

Sentence Builder Prepositions at the end of sentences

2 **Read the text and complete the question and answers. Finish all your questions and answers with a preposition.**

> Mark works for a newspaper, *The Daily Voice*. He likes his job and he likes the people he works with because they all like the same things as him. They are all keen on sport and watching different types of films. Their names are Julia, Jake and Rupert.
>
> At the moment, Mark is talking on the phone. He is talking to an explorer, Ralph Stevenson. The explorer is famous because he has just walked from Cape Town, in the south of Africa, to Tangiers, in the north. Mark and the explorer are going to meet up. Mark's going to interview him and write a story about him.

1 Who does *Mark work for*?
The Daily Voice.

2 What is *The Daily Voice*?
It's the newspaper that Mark _____.

3 What are they all _____?
Sport and watching different types of films.

4 Who is Mark _____?
The explorer Ralph Stevenson.

5 What is Ralph _____?
For walking from the south of Africa to the north.

6 What is Mark going to _____?
Ralph Stevenson's travels.

Word Builder Prefixes

3 **Complete the words with the correct prefix.**

1 We'll never escape. It's *im*possible.

2 There's a very ___pleasant smell outside. Close the windows, quickly.

3 I'm afraid I ___agree with you about women's rights.

4 It's ___legal to drive when you're under seventeen.

5 Sometimes, I'd like to be able to be ___visible and ___appear.

6 When can we ___wrap our presents?

7 Get ___dressed, put your pyjamas on, clean your teeth and go to bed.

8 We have to learn fifty ___regular past forms for a test.

LESSON

18

GRAMMAR
Question tags

1 * Look at the pictures (a–d). Match them with sentences (1–4).

a 3

b ☐

c ☐

d ☐

1 You haven't been learning long, have you?
2 But you're against child labour, aren't you?
3 Our new teacher's American, isn't he?
4 'You believe in freedom of speech, don't you?' 'Not during an exam.'

2 * Complete the questions with the correct question tags.

1 You're in class 12C, *are you/aren't you*?
2 We aren't lost, *are we/aren't we*?
3 Pete loves reggae, *does he/doesn't he*?
4 The train doesn't leave until 9 p.m. *does it/doesn't it*?
5 You haven't heard this CD yet, *have you/haven't you*?
6 Sally's eyes are really dark, *isn't she/aren't they*?
7 Paul will meet us at the station *will he/won't he*?
8 That test was really difficult, *was it/wasn't it*?
9 You weren't sleeping when I phoned, *were you/weren't you*?
10 I can go out tonight, *can I/can't I*?

3 ** Complete the dialogue with the correct question tags.

A: Look, there's going to be a guest speaker in the school hall today. Jack Ireland.
B: He's the footballer, ¹ *isn't he* ?
A: You're joking, ² _____?
B: What do you mean?
A: I mean, you didn't really think he was a footballer, ³ _____?
B: Why not?
A: Look at the photo. He isn't very sporty, ⁴ _____? And he looks a bit old to be a footballer, ⁵ _____?
B: I suppose so. So who is he?
A: He's an explorer. You remember those people who walked to the North Pole last year, ⁶ _____?
B: Yes. They started in Canada, ⁷ _____?
A: That's right. Well, Jack Ireland was the leader of the group.
B: So, what's he doing here?
A: I don't know. We'll find out, ⁸ _____? Come on, let's go to the school hall and get a seat.
B: There aren't many people here, ⁹ _____?
A: That's because lessons haven't finished yet, ¹⁰ _____?
B: What if someone sees us? What will we say?
A: We'll tell the truth. We were coming back from the library, ¹¹ _____?
B: We'll get into trouble.
A: No we won't. We're in year twelve now. We had a free lesson. We can go where we like during free lessons, ¹² _____? Don't worry so much. I wouldn't get you into trouble, ¹³ _____?
B: I suppose not.

4 *** Rewrite the questions with the same meaning as the one above.

1 Is that Tom?
That's _____ *Tom, isn't it* _____?
2 Will you come to the cinema with me?
You _____?
3 Were you having a bath when I phoned?
You weren't _____?
4 Is the shop open on Sundays?
The shop _____?
5 Has your sister got a car?
Your sister _____?
6 Is this where your dad works?
This _____?
7 Doesn't Matt want to come with us?
Matt doesn't _____?
8 Did we watch this film last week?
We _____?

51

Workshop 3

Writing

❶ Look at the start and finish of a review of the book *To Kill a Mockingbird* and complete it with the words below.

best-seller   by   drama   made   recommend   set   since   sum up   would   ~~written~~

To Kill a Mockingbird was [1]___written___
[2]_____ Harper Lee in 1960 and
is a [3]_____ and mystery
[4]_____ in the southern United
States in the 1930s. It was a
[5]_____ when it came out, and
[6]_____ then it has sold over thirty
million copies. A film was [7]_____
of the book in 1962 which won three
Oscars.
....

To [8]_____, the book is an
exciting, sometimes happy and
sometimes sad, story of life in a small
town in the United States before
the Second World War. If you enjoy
historical dramas, social reform and
mystery, I [9]_____ definitely
[10]_____ reading this
classic story.

❷ Look at the opinions of the characters and plot and choose the correct words to complete the sentences.

1 The story is told by six-year-old Scout Finch. It is very well written *though*/*however*/*also* it doesn't really sound as if it is such a young child talking.

2 *As well as*/*Addition*/*Another* criticism that can be made of the book is that the characters of the people in the town are a bit two-dimensional.

3 The plot is full of *both*/*also*/*not only* excitement and mystery.

4 Atticus Finch is *not only*/*both*/*also* a social reformer but also a warm and caring father.

5 Boo Radley is a little bit scary *both*/*not only*/*as well as* being sad.

❸ Choose a book you have had to read for school. Use Exercises 1 and 2 to help you write a review of the book. Write between 120 and 180 words.

Speaking

❶ 1.43 Look at the picture and think about what you can see. Then complete the conversation with the words below and listen to check.

~~be~~   probably   think (x 2)   looks (x 2)   sort   have   kind   background

A: So, can you tell me something about this picture?

B: Well, it's a picture of a woman and two men. She must [1]___be___ in her mid thirties. He [2]_____ younger.

A: Where do you think she's probably from?

B: Well, she's wearing a [3]_____ of dress and, looking at her hair, she's [4]_____ a Native American Indian.

A: And what sort of person do you think she is?

B: She [5]_____ strong, I [6]_____. She must know a lot about the area. She also looks a helpful [7]_____of person.

A: Where do you think they are?

B: There are mountains in the [8]_____ so it's probably in the Rocky Mountains in the USA. Perhaps the men are trying to find a way through the mountains.

A: What do you think has happened?

B: I think they've had some sort of problem. She might [9]_____ helped them to escape from some other Native Americans.

A: And why do you think she might be a heroine?

B: I've heard stories of a Native American woman who helped two explorers cross the USA. She'd be a very useful person to know, I [10]_____.

Check Your Progress 6

① Biography Complete the words.

Kinds of hero
1 I_b___t__
2 p__n___

Kinds of families
3 a___t__r___c
4 p__v___g__

Things you can join
5 c___l s_r__c_
6 the a___

Things you can study
7 m___c___
8 l__

Things you can campaign for
9 e___l r__h__
10 f___d__ of s___c_

Things you can campaign against
11 p___r__
12 c__l_ l_b___

/12

② Prefixes Complete the text with the correct form of the words in brackets.

My friend thinks it would be good to be famous. She says we are [1]_____ (visible) now and that famous people have much better lives because everyone knows who they are.
I [2]_____ (agree). I think it would be really [3]_____ (pleasant) to be famous. You can never [4]_____ (appear) from view. It's just [5]_____ (possible) to lead a normal life. Someone will always recognise you and ask you for your photo or want to talk to you. I'm sure most people are nice but, if famous people are tired or in a hurry, their 'fans' soon become [6]_____ (friendly) and [7]_____ (sympathetic) and will probably go straight to a newspaper to tell them how rude their 'hero' was. And then there's the paparazzi. It should be [8]_____ (legal) to take secret photos of people. That must be awful.

/8

③ Speculating about the past Complete the sentences with the correct modal; *must, might* or *can't* and a verb in the correct form.

1 Mike / see / an Indiana Jones film. He loves action films.
Mike must have seen an Indiana Jones film.
2 Jackie / be / abroad. She hasn't even got a passport.
Jackie _____ abroad.
3 Perhaps Louisa / play / the Lara Croft computer game. She liked the film.
Perhaps Louisa _____ the Lara Croft computer game.
4 Sam / meet / some famous people. His mum's a journalist.
Sam _____ some famous people.
5 Sue / read / a James Bond book. Everyone has.
Sue _____ a James Bond book.
6 Terry / fall / in love. He's only interested in computer games!
Terry _____ in love.

/5

④ Question tags Match the beginnings (1-5) with the correct question tags (a-e).

1 You've heard of Zorro, ___   a was he?
2 Your dad wasn't angry, ___   b have you?
3 You don't want to go out again, ___   c haven't you?
4 You haven't joined the army, ___   d do you?
5 Your grandfather fought for equal rights ___   e didn't he?

/5

TOTAL SCORE   /30

Module Diary

① Look at the objectives on page 45 in the Students' Book. Choose three and evaluate your learning.

1 Now I can _____
well / quite well / with problems.
2 Now I can _____
well / quite well / with problems.
3 Now I can _____
well / quite well / with problems

② Look at your results. What language areas in this module do you need to study more?

Exam Choice 3

Reading

1 **Read the text quickly and match the names (1-6) with the facts (a-f).**

1 John Kennedy ___
2 William Hague ___
3 Gordon Brown ___
4 Luiz Inacio Lula da Silva ___
5 Richard Nixon ___
6 David Cameron ___

a Leader of the British Labour Party after Tony Blair.
b Lost the 1960 American election.
c The most popular President in the world when he was leader.
d The leader of the British Conservative Party in 2008.
e The leader of the British Conservative Party In 1997.
f He became President in 1960.

How **important** is image?

In the past, politicians needed to be serious, intelligent and honest. ¹_____ That all changed in 1960. John Kennedy and Richard Nixon were both trying to become President of the USA. Before the election, they met for a debate. People listening to this on the radio agreed that Richard Nixon had been the better speaker. However, the people who watched it on TV had a very different opinion. They felt that Kennedy was the more impressive speaker. Why? ²_____ He was younger, better-looking and his suit was more fashionable. He looked at the camera when he spoke and he knew when to smile, when to look serious and when to look sad. In the end, he became President and many people say that his TV performance was the reason why.

Since then, looks and image have become more and more important. Elections have become more like *Big Brother* than a serious political event. Parties have chosen younger and younger leaders hoping that they will become the 'new' Kennedy. ³_____

In 1997, Tony Blair had just become the leader of Britain. He was handsome, young and had a nice smile. The Conservative Party chose a new leader, William Hague. ⁴_____ However, when he tried to become more popular with young people, it was a disaster. He appeared in public in a baseball cap. It might work now but, in 1997, the country wasn't ready for such an image.

By 2008, Tony Blair had gone. The new labour leader was Gordon Brown, the complete opposite of Blair. He was overweight, didn't know when to smile and didn't look natural when he tried. ⁵_____ The Conservatives had chosen a younger man, David Cameron, as their leader. In the summer, both leaders had their photos taken on holiday. Gordon Brown was still in his jacket and formal trousers although he had taken his tie off. David Cameron was on the beach in shorts and an old T-shirt. This casual image was much more popular and he became Prime Minister two years later.

However, image and youth aren't always the most important things. From 2003 until 2011, the most popular president in the world was a man in his late fifties to mid sixties. He had grey hair and a beard and was slightly plump. He wore traditional, dark suits, often with a white shirt and a red tie. While president, 80 percent of his people were happy with him. ⁶_____ They liked him because he worked for them and did what he promised. His name? Luiz Inacio Lula da Silva of Brazil.

2 Read the text again. Match the sentences (a–f) with gaps (1–6) in the text. There is one extra sentence.

a He was even younger.
b That's why people like this new style of politician.
c They weren't interested in what he looked like.
d Because he looked better.
e It doesn't always work.
f No one cared what they looked like.
g He also wore dark, old-fashioned suits.

Speaking

3 **1.44** Read a student's answer in an exam and complete what they say with the words below. Then listen to check.

background   in   kind   look   looks   maybe   must
of   opinion   probably   think

A: For the next part of the exam, I'd like you to look at two pictures. They show two different heroes. I'd like you to say what you think they did and what kind of people they were.

B: The first picture is of a man. He ¹_____ be in his mid fifties. He's wearing a ²_____ of uniform. He's ³_____ a soldier. He ⁴_____ very strong and not very friendly. There's a desert in the ⁵_____. ⁶_____ it's Iraq or Afghanistan but it was taken a long time ago, I ⁷_____.
The second person is a woman. She looks very kind. ⁸_____ the background, I can see a room with children in it. They ⁹_____ very poor. In my ¹⁰_____, she's probably a nurse or maybe some sort ¹¹_____ social reformer helping to stop child labour.

Listening

4 **1.45** Listen to two people discussing a hero and choose the best answers.

1 What is Amy's problem?
  a She doesn't know anything about Churchill or Napoleon.
  b She doesn't like History.
  c She doesn't know who to write about.

2 What does Amy know about Douglas Bader?
  a nothing
  b a lot
  c Only that he flew across the Atlantic.

3 What was amazing about Douglas Bader after the crash?
  a That he didn't die.
  b That he learned to walk again.
  c That he took so long to walk again.

4 When did Douglas Bader start flying again?
  a Before the war started.
  b At the start of the war.
  c A year after the war had started.

5 Where did he get legs from in Germany?
  a The Germans made them.
  b The Germans found his old ones.
  c The Germans allowed the British to drop some new legs from a plane.

6 What does Amy think about Douglas Bader now?
  a That he's a real hero and she will write about him.
  b That he's a real hero but she won't write about him.
  c That he isn't really a hero.

7 Where will they watch the film?
  a on television at Rory's house
  b on television at Amy's house
  c on Amy's laptop

Exam Choice 3

Use of English

5 **Put the words in brackets into the correct form.**

William Wilberforce is famous as someone who fought against [1]_____ (SLAVE) and helped to make it [2]_____ (LEGAL) in Britain. He was born into a [3]_____ (WEALTH) family in the north of England and studied at Cambridge University. While there, he was more interested in having a good time than in studying or worrying about other people. However, when he was still in his [4]_____ (TWENTY) he went on a tour of Europe and when he returned, he had changed.

He helped to change the law and was against [5]_____ (RACE) which was quite unusual at the time he lived. He also tried to help other people. He understood that education could help to reduce [6]_____ (POOR) and he gave money for special Sunday schools for poor people. He was a kind, generous man and he found it [7]_____ (POSSIBLE) to get rid of people who worked for him, even when they were old and couldn't do their jobs properly.

There were some things he [8]_____ (AGREE) with, though. He didn't like protest marches or [9]_____ (DEMONSTRATE) by workers and he was also against [10]_____ (WOMAN) rights. However, this wasn't surprising for someone born in 1759 and we should remember him for the good things he did rather than the things that he didn't do.

Writing

6 **Complete the email with the verbs *help, like, make* and *want* in the correct form.**

From:	Neil
To:	Steve

Hi Steve

My mum [1]_____ me to have my hair cut. Well, what I mean is that she's going to [2]_____ me have it cut if I don't go soon. I'd [3]_____ the hairdresser to give me a cool style, not just 'normal' short hair. The trouble is, I need someone [4]_____ me decide which style would be best. Have you got any ideas of whose images to 'google' for some ideas?

Thanks

Neil

7 **Choose one of the situations below. First write a note and then write the reply.**

- Someone wants you to do something or is making you do something (what?) and you want some advice or help

- You want to ask someone to go somewhere with you (where?)

Write between 50 and 80 words for the note and the reply.

ADVENTURE

TOPIC TALK – VOCABULARY

1 Complete the activities. Use the pictures to help you.

1 k_ayaking_

2 b_____

3 h_____

4 s_____

5 s_____

6 c_____

7 s_____

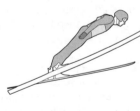

8 s_____
j_____

2 Complete the sentences with the words below.

caving cliff India motorbike river

1 I climbed a __cliff__.
2 Jamie dived into a _____.
3 Mandy went on a _____.
4 Sally went _____.
5 Chris travelled to _____.

3 Add vowels (*a,e,i,o,u*) to complete the words.

1 The scuba dive was _a_ w _e_ s _o_ m _e_.
2 Hiking is really _ x h _ l _ r _ t _ n g
3 Surfing is g r _ _ t f _ n.
4 Wow! Kayaking here is _ n c r _ d _ b l _.
5 Snowboarding is the _ l t _ m _ t _ t h r _ l l.
6 I was a b _ t f r _ g h t _ n _d at first but I love skiing now.
7 You looked r _ _ l l y s c _ r _ d when the roller coaster started.
8 My mum was p _ t r _ f _ _ d when my dad took her sailing.
9 Mark never goes skiing because he is s c _ r _ d s t _ f f of breaking his leg.
10 I didn't enjoy snorkelling. I was t _ r r _ f _ _ d that a shark would eat me.

4 Complete the sentences with the words and phrases below.

ever incredible most ~~love~~ exciting way rather scared when who

1 I'd __love__ to go snowboarding.
2 I would _____ go surfing than sailing.
3 The _____ _____ experience I've _____ had was _____ I went sky diving. It was _____. I was _____ at first but then I started to enjoy it.
4 There is no _____ I would ever go canyoning. I think people _____ go canyoning are crazy.

5 Complete the words and then make the sentences true for you.

There's no [1]w _ay_____ I would [2]e_____ go _____.
I'd [3]l_____ to go _____.
I would [4]r_____ go _____ than skiing.
I [5]t_____ people [6]w_____ go _____ are crazy.
The most exciting [7]e_____ I have [8]e_____ had was [9]w_____ I_____. It [10]w_____ _____.

Steve Backshall is a TV presenter and writer who is famous for his programmes about wild places and animals around the world.

1 *D* Steve loves adventure and outdoor activities. He is a great climber and he is also passionate about kayaking, cycling and, of course, wild animals. But, he is always very careful and he doesn't do anything he isn't trained for. So to answer the question, in his opinion none of the activities he does are risky if you know what you are doing.

2 ___ It was probably when he was in the desert. He hadn't had any water for over a day. Suddenly, he saw a pool and dived in. Unfortunately, there was a rock under the surface and he hit his head badly. It took him four days to get to a hospital. It showed him that there are always risks and you have to be careful at all times.

Here are a few of his best shows.

REALLY WILD SHOW

3 ___ *The Really Wild Show* was a television show about animals. Two people in London talked to animal experts and looked at animals they had brought in and another presenter travelled around the world looking at the same animals in the wild. Steve Backshall was one of these people and he went on journeys to Africa and other countries.

4 ___ The programme was one of the best and most popular children's shows on the BBC and it lasted from 1986 until 2006 with several different presenters during that time. So, it's not on TV anymore, but there are so many satellite TV channels showing old programmes, I'm sure you can still see the shows quite often.

DEADLY 60

5 ___ Well, *Deadly 60* is shown on CBBC, the BBC's children's channel. Most programmes on CBBC are for six to twelve year olds but anyone interested in learning about dangerous animals will love *Deadly 60* because Steve Backshall is such a great presenter. So, the answer to the question is for children, teenagers and adults.

6 ___ In a word, very. Each programme is twenty-eight minutes long and shows four or five animals. That means there is enough time to show how they live and why they are dangerous but without getting too boring. You can now see it on *Animal Planet*, too, so they must think the programme is worth watching as well.

7 ___ Lots and he always tries to hold them or goes close to them to get a good film. He has been kayaking in rivers in Africa full of crocodiles and he has dived with sharks. Once, in South America, a crocodile bit him on the leg while he was looking for snakes in a river.

LOST LAND OF THE VOLCANO

8 ___ Steve joined some other explorers in the caves inside a volcano in New Guinea. When they were inside, Steve suddenly became ill. His temperature rose to over 40⁰C and he spent the night lying on the cold, wet ground. No one could carry him. He had to get out on his own or he might have died. In the end, it took him ten hours and he was ill for a long time after leaving the volcano.

1 Read the text on the left quickly and match the events (1–4) with the places (a–d).

1 He hit his head badly _b_
2 He went kayaking in a river full of crocodiles ___
3 A crocodile bit his leg ___
4 He was very ill with a temperature of over 40⁰C ___

a in South America.
b in the desert.
c in New Guinea.
d in Africa.

2 Read the text again. Match the questions (A–I) with the gaps (1–8) in the text. There is one extra question.

A What was it about?
B Why was his life in danger?
C What dangerous animals does he meet?
D Does he like taking risks?
E How long has he been making the show?
F Is it still on TV?
G What has been the worst thing that has happened to him?
H How good is it?
I Who is it for?

Word Builder Confusing nouns

3 Choose the correct words to complete the sentences.

1 There's only one bed here so I have to sleep on the *floor*/*ground* in the living room.
2 We went on a day *journey*/*trip* to visit a castle.
3 When Magellan sailed around the world, his *voyage*/*flight* lasted for three years.
4 Don't dive into the lake. You might hit your head on something under the *ground*/*surface*.
5 There was a lot of snow at the airport so our *voyage*/*flight* was three hours late.
6 The train was very comfortable and we had a very nice *journey*/*travel*.
7 Don't put your tent here. The *floor*/*ground* is very hard here.

Sentence Builder Prepositions + *-ing* forms

4 Complete the sentences with the correct form of the verb in brackets and a preposition where necessary.

1 Thanks _*for telling*_ me about this new wildlife programme. (tell)
2 I've always been interested _____ about dangerous animals. (learn)
3 Do you think he was worried _____ in the Amazon? (kayak)
4 They spent three days in the forests of India without _____ any tigers. (see)
5 We had to learn a lot about snakes _____ to catch them. (try)
6 Aren't you bored _____ the same programme again and again? (watch)
7 The animal wasn't dangerous and it went away _____ them. (attack)
8 Dinner wasn't ready, so I watched the programme _____ dinner. (have)

Writing

5 Read the instructions below. Write the email.

Introduction:
Thank your friend for sending *(What? a present, an email, a text, a letter)* and write a short sentence about it.

Your news:
You are on holiday *(where?)*. Tell your friend about the journey and what you are doing at the moment. Mention things you've done on the holiday and your plans for the next few days.

Ending:
Give a reason why you have to finish the email *(Why? your parents, a trip, it's late at night, you want to go swimming)* and say goodbye.

REMEMBER

Complete exercises A-B before you start this lesson.

A Complete the sentences with *will, may* or *be going to* and the verb in brackets in the correct form. Use each form once in each group of three sentences.

1 **a** Look out. That rock *is going to fall*. (fall)

b I think that you _____ kayaking. (enjoy)

c Bring some sandwiches because the café _____ closed. It sometimes is. (be)

2 **a** I don't know if I can meet you tomorrow. We _____ sailing but I don't know yet. (go)

b What new extreme sport do you think _____ popular next year? (be)

c He's going too fast. He _____! (crash)

B Look at the holiday plans and complete the information with the correct verbs in the Present Continuous.

> Holiday all booked! (us and Uncle Albert)
> Leave home 2 p.m., Thursday 16 May
> Meet Uncle Albert at the airport.
> Fly to Dublin by plane.
> Stay at the Mount Royal Hotel (I don't have to share a room with anyone!)

1 We ___ *are going* ___ on holiday to Dublin.

2 We _____ at 2 p.m. on Thursday 16 May.

3 Uncle Albert _____ us at the airport.

4 We _____ to Dublin by plane.

5 We _____ at the Mount Royal Hotel.

6 I _____ a room with my parents or Uncle Albert.

7 I _____ in my own room.

1 * Choose the correct words to complete the sentences.

1 **A:** We need one more person for our sailing trip tomorrow.

B: Oh, okay. *I'll go*/I'm going.

2 **A:** The skiing holiday cost €500 last year.

B: I'm sure it *may be/will be* more expensive this year.

3 **A:** Why are you taking so many clothes with you?

B: Well, it *is going to be/may be* cold and, if it isn't, they aren't very heavy.

4 **A:** I hope you don't break your leg again when you go on your winter holidays.

B: Don't worry. I'*m going to be/'m being* more careful this time.

5 **A:** Do you want to go swimming this afternoon?

B: I can't. I *meet/'m meeting* Eleanor at 3 o'clock.

6 **A:** It's crazy. Our train *arrives/is arriving* at 8 p.m.

B: What's wrong with that?

A: The last bus *leaves/is leaving* the station at 7.55.

2 ** Complete the dialogue with the phrases below.

> doesn't leave   going to go   going to have   'll be   'll eat
> 'll pay   'll phone   'm meeting   ~~may be late~~   will cost

Stella: Hi, mum. It's me. I ¹ *may be late* home today. I'm not sure yet but don't worry.

Mum: Oh dear. How will I know when to get your dinner ready?

Stella: I ² _____ you when I know exactly what time I ³ _____ home.

Mum: Thank you. We're ⁴ _____ fish tonight.

Stella: Lovely!

Stella: Hi, mum. It's me again. I'm at the station but the next train ⁵ _____ until 10 p.m.

Mum: Ten o'clock! Get a taxi. I ⁶ _____ for it.

Stella: A taxi! It ⁷ _____ more than a hundred pounds.

Stella: Hi, mum. It's me again.

Mum: Where are you?

Stella: I'm still in London. I phoned Lucy. I ⁸ _____ her in ten minutes and we're ⁹ _____ to a restaurant for something to eat while we wait for the train.

Mum: What about your fish?

Stella: Don't worry. I ¹⁰ _____ it tomorrow.

3 *** Complete the dialogues with the verbs in brackets in the best form. Use *may, will, be going to*, Present Continuous or Present Simple

A: We should book our holiday soon. We need to decide where to go.

B: Okay, I ¹____'ll____ (switch on) the computer and we can look on the internet. We ²_____ (find) something interesting.

A: Do you know anything about Slovenia?

B: Nothing.

A: Nor do I but it ³_____ (be) a good place to go.

B: Possibly. Have a look. I ⁴_____ (be) back in a minute.

A: Where are you going?

B: To the kitchen. I ⁵_____ (make) a cup of tea. Do you want one?

A: Yes, please.

B: Look. There's a plane to Ljubljana on 21 July. It ⁶_____ (leave) at 3 p.m. and the tickets are only £60 each.

A: What time ⁷_____ (it / arrive)?

B: It ⁸_____ (arrive) at half past six.

A: Have you packed yet?

B: No. What ⁹_____ (the weather / be) like?

A: Hot and sunny. It's near Italy.

B: ¹⁰_____ (it / be) expensive?

A: I don't know. It ¹¹_____ (be) but don't worry.

B: How much money ¹²_____ (you / take)?

A: About €200. I ¹³_____ (not / take) my credit card. I ¹⁴_____ (be) careful this year!

Grammar Alive Plans and predictions

4 Use the prompts to complete the conversation.

A: I / go on holiday tomorrow.
I'm going on holiday tomorrow.

B: Really. you / go / alone?
¹ *Are you going to go alone?*

A: No, I / go / with Jack and Tommy.
²_____

B: Where / you / go?
³_____

A: We / go / to Scotland.
⁴_____

B: How / you / get there?
⁵_____

A: By train. It / leave at six o'clock in the morning.
⁶_____

B: I hope you wake up!

A: Don't worry. My mum / wake me up.
⁷_____

B: Have you booked a hotel?

A: No. We / sleep in a tent.
⁸_____

B: A tent! In Scotland! You / be / cold!
⁹_____

A: Not tomorrow. The weather forecast says it / be / warm and sunny all day.
¹⁰_____

B: Well, it / be sunny tomorrow but it / not / be sunny for long. It never is in Scotland.
¹¹_____

61

SKILLS
Listening

1 Look at the list of activities and the descriptions of the three people. Then answer the questions.

do a bungee jump   fly in an ultra light plane
go canyoning down a waterfall
~~go on a canoe safari~~
go white water rafting down some rapids
go sea kayaking along the coast   go trekking
go on a zip-line above the rain forest

Bob is scared of heights and flying

Natasha can't swim and is scared of water.

Andy is scared of heights and water.

1 Which activities could Bob do?
go on a canoe safari , _____ , _____ , _____

2 Which activities would be good for Natasha?
_____ , _____ , _____ , _____

3 Which activity would none of the three people like? _____

4 Which is the only activity they could do together? _____

Talk Builder Asking for information

2 **2.1** Match questions (1-8) with the correct answers (a-h). Then listen to check your answers.

1 Sorry, what does BASE jumping mean? _d_

2 Have you got any information about high-lining? ___

3 Excuse me, could you give me some information about extreme sports? ___

4 Can you tell me where the snorkelling club is, please? ___

5 I'm going hiking tomorrow and I need some new boots. Have you got any? ___

6 What activities would you recommend for a teenager who doesn't want to do anything too dangerous? ___

7 I'm sorry but what is extreme skiing exactly? ___

8 Do you know where I can do sea kayaking? ___

a Of course. What would you like to know about them?

b No, I'm sorry. I'm afraid I haven't. But here are the names and addresses of some local sports shops.

c Our canoe safaris are very interesting and safe.

d It's the sport of jumping off buildings with a parachute.

e Yes. There are several places on the coast which offer lessons and rent boats.

f It's the same as skiing but you do it away from the normal ski areas in much more difficult and dangerous places.

g Yes, we've got this brochure and there's more about it on our website.

h Certainly. It's on the beach next to the café.

3 **2.2** Choose the correct words to complete the sentences. Then decide who says each one; the customer (C) or the person working in the tourist information office (W). Listen to check your answers.

1 *Could/Do/Did* you give me some information about the island, please? _C_

2 What would you *want/need/like* to know? ___

3 I'd like some *recommendation/brochure/information* about adventure sports, please. ___

4 Erm, well, we've got various *brochures/information/help* here ... ___

5 Could you tell me *of/about/some* extreme sports, please? ___

6 Sorry. What does 'bungee jumping' *do/work/mean*? ___

7 What *exactly is/means/does* BASE jumping? ___

8 Do you know *how/who/where* I can do BASE jumping? ___

9 Have you got any *help/recommendation/information* about it? ___

10 I'm afraid I *don't/won't/can't* help you. ___

11 Can you tell me *where/whose/what* it is, please? ___

12 No *sorry/problem/I can't*. It's just down the street next to the church. ___

Check Your Progress 7

1 Adventure **Match the beginnings (1–10) with the endings (a–h) to make eight activities.**

1 BASE ___
2 BMX ___
3 extreme ___
4 round the world ___
5 high ___
6 go ___
7 rock ___
8 scuba ___

a climbing
b diving
c sailing
d jumping
e lining
f riding
g skiing
h surfing

/8

2 Confusing nouns **Complete the sentences with one word.**

1 I'm going on the school t_____ next month.
2 I enjoyed our holiday except for the j_____ home which was awful.
3 Some teams travelled to the first World Cup by boat. The v_____ took a long time.
4 Don't sit on the g_____. You'll get wet.
5 We went to Australia by plane. The f_____ took twenty-four hours.
6 What is the cheapest form of public t_____ in your country? Buses or trains?
7 The fish are coming to the s_____ of the water to get food.

/7

3 Predictions, intentions and arrangements **Put the verbs in brackets into the correct form using** will, may, be going to, **Present Continuous or Present Simple.**

A: I've arranged to meet Mick tomorrow.
B: What time ¹_____ (you / meet) him?
A: I don't know. He ²_____ (phone) me when he finishes work.
A: We're getting the train to London tomorrow. Do you want to come?
B: What time ³_____ (the train / leave)?
A: We ⁴_____ (try) to get the 7:30 a.m. train.
B: What ⁵_____ (you / do) in London?
A: I'm not sure. We ⁶_____ (go) to the zoo but we ⁷_____ (not go) there if it's raining.

/7

4 Asking for information **Complete the conversation with the words below. There are three extra words.**

about afraid any course exactly excuse like mean sorry want with

A: ¹_____ me, could you give me some information ²_____ surfing lessons, please?
B: Of ³_____. What do you want to know?
A: I'd ⁴_____ to know what different kinds of surfing you can learn.
B: Well, there's body surfing.
A: I'm ⁵_____. What is body surfing, ⁶_____?
B: It's where you lie down on the board. It's easier than standing up.
A: Have you got ⁷_____ information about courses, please?
B: Yes, I've got a brochure here somewhere. Here you are. There are courses for beginners and more experienced surfers and for juniors and adults.
A: What does 'junior' ⁸_____?
B: People aged between twelve and sixteen. There are no courses for under twelves.

/8

TOTAL SCORE **/30**

Module Diary

1 **Look at the objectives on page 53 in the Students' Book. Choose three and evaluate your learning.**

1 Now I can _____
well / quite well / with problems.
2 Now I can _____
well / quite well / with problems.
3 Now I can _____
well / quite well / with problems.

2 **Look at your results. What language areas in this module do you need to study more?**

Sound Choice 4

1 **2.4** Grammar - contractions **Listen to the sentences and repeat them.**

1 I won't go bungee jumping again.
2 I'll meet you outside the post office.
3 You mustn't use your phone in here.
4 Tommy can't count to ten in German yet.
5 My dad doesn't often get angry.
6 There aren't any snorkelling lessons this week.

2 **2.4** Grammar - contractions **Listen again to the sentences in exercise 1 and write the word in each sentence which includes a contraction.**

1 _won't_   4 _____
2 _____   5 _____
3 _____   6 _____

3 **2.5** Grammar - intonation in question tags **Listen to the questions. Write K if the speaker knows the answer already. Write NS, if the speaker isn't sure of the answer.**

1 _K_   4 _____
2 _____ 5 _____
3 _____ 6 _____

4 **2.5** Grammar - intonation in question tags **Listen again and repeat the sentences with the correct intonation.**

1 You're the new student, aren't you?
2 You're new here, aren't you?
3 You go surfing, don't you?
4 You like heavy metal, don't you?
5 This isn't your bag, is it?
6 This isn't the right address, is it?

5 **2.6** Consonants - consonant clusters at the end of words **Say the words. Then listen and repeat the endings and the complete words.**

1 racism   6 myths
2 scientists   7 risk
3 friend   8 equipment
4 privileged   9 ground
5 experience

6 **2.7** Vowels **Decide which word in each set of three has a different vowel sound then listen to check.**

1 poor, born, (hot)   4 royal, voyage, bought
2 not, proud, poverty   5 frost, about, crowds
3 boil, ground, cloudy   6 snorkel, cost, floor

7 **2.8** Spelling - vowels **Look at the words with the same vowels. Decide which pairs of words have the same vowel sound and which word in each group has no pair. Then listen to check.**

ou: fought, could, thousands, country, bought, without, would, labour, journey
oo: poor, school, floor, pool, childhood
oa: board, coast, boat
oi: noise, going, coin

8 **2.9** Expressions **Listen to the underlined words and repeat them. Then listen to the complete sentences and repeat them.**

1 Could you give me some information about skiing?
2 What activities do you recommend?
3 What does BASE jumping mean?
4 I'm sorry, but what is high-lining exactly?
5 Have you got any information about BMX riding?

TOPIC TALK – VOCABULARY

1 Complete the types of climate with the correct letters.

1 **Great Britain:** m _i_ l _d_, t _ _ p _ r _ _ _
Warm summers (20-25°C) and cool winters (0-10°C). There is no wet or dry season. It can rain at any time of the year.

2 **Italy:** M _ _ _ t _ r _ _ n _ _ _
Hot, dry summers (30-35°C) and cool, wet winters (5-15°C). There is very little rain in the summer but quite a lot in the winter.

3 **The Canary Islands:** s _ _ - t _ _ p _ c _ _
Hot, dry summers (30-35°C) and warm, wet winters (12-20°C).

4 **Sudan:** d _ s _ r _
Very hot and dry summers (30-40°C). Warm, dry winters (15-20°C). There is very little rain at any time of the year.

5 **Congo:** e _ _ _ t _ r _ _ _, t _ _ p _ c _ _
Hot and wet all the year round (25-35°C). There are no real different seasons.

2 Label the pictures.

1 b_each_

2 m_____

3 c_____

4 d_____

5 l_____

6 v_____

7 m_____

8 p_____

9 f_____

3 Match the beginnings with the correct endings.

Problems

1 noise _d_	a jams
2 climate ___	b fumes
3 CO$_2$ ___	c of species
4 extinction ___	d pollution
5 extreme ___	e fires
6 forest ___	f change
7 exhaust ___	g emissions
8 traffic ___	h weather

Solutions

1 save ___	a turbines
2 solar ___	b transport
3 wind ___	c consumption
4 share ___	d trees
5 public ___	e energy
6 plant ___	f cars
7 reduce ___	g panels

4 Complete the conversation with the words below.

~~climate~~ cycle degrees hills landscape litter problems rarely recycle solutions temperate temperature

A: What's the ¹___ _climate_ ___ like in your country?

B: My country has a ²_____ climate. In the summer, the ³_____ is usually about 20°C and, in the winter, it ⁴_____ drops below zero ⁵_____.

A: Describe the ⁶_____ near your home.

B: There are a few ⁷_____ but they aren't very high, and there's a small forest and a lake.

A: Are there any ⁸_____ in your area?

B: The worst is ⁹_____. The town centre is full of it, especially on a Saturday night. We also have bad traffic jams.

A: Can you think of any ¹⁰_____ for these problems?

B: It's difficult. People should ¹¹_____ all their waste. I always throw my rubbish away properly. The problem with cars is that the roads are very dangerous. I would like to ¹²_____ to school but I go by car with my mum.

22 GRAMMAR
Future Continuous

REMEMBER

Complete exercises A–B before you start lesson 24, page 69.

A Complete the dialogues with the pronouns below.

> her   hers   ~~him~~   his   it   me   mine   ours
> theirs   them   us   yours

A: Who's that boy over there?
B: Don't you know ¹_*him*_? That's Peter Davies. He's in year twelve. You know the painting in the hall?
A: Yes.
B: It's ²_____. He painted ³_____.
A: Where are Ted and Lorna?
B: I haven't seen ⁴_____. Why?
A: I think these bags are ⁵_____.
B: No, they aren't. They're ⁶_____. I've been shopping all morning.
A: I'm glad we made this website together. I couldn't have done it on my own.
B: Maria did. ⁷_____ is great.
A: Not as good as ⁸_____. I'm really proud of what we've done. Well, what you've done. The website is ⁹_____ really.
B: Hey, it wasn't just ¹⁰_____. You did a lot as well.
A: You're right. We're a team. Maybe Mrs Jones will ask ¹¹_____ to help ¹²_____ with the school website.

B Choose the correct words to complete the texts.

When I walked into the room, I didn't see ¹*anyone/ no one/someone*. Then, suddenly, I heard ²*everything/something/anything*. The lights went on and ³ *anyone/someone/everyone* shouted 'Happy Birthday!' as loudly as they could. It was a great surprise.

I was bored last week. I didn't have ⁴*nothing/ anything/something* to do. I phoned a few friends but ⁵*no one/anyone/everyone* answered. I switched on the TV but there was ⁶*something/ anything/nothing* interesting on. In the end, I sent emails to ⁷*someone/everyone/anyone* in my address book. It took a long time because I wrote ⁸*something/anything/nothing* different to each of them.

❶ * Complete the sentences with the Future Continuous form of the verbs in brackets.

1 We're doing a project on the environment at school this month. Next Tuesday morning, we *will be planting* (plant) trees in the park.
2 Meet me in the café. I _____ (sit) next to the window.
3 Look at this rain. We _____ (not swim) today.
4 I _____ (not travel) by bus to the cinema. I _____ (cycle).
5 What _____ (you wear) to the party next week?
6 I've got to hurry. My parents _____ (wait) for me.
7 I can't go out tonight. I _____ (study) all evening.
8 _____ (you use) your laptop this morning or can I borrow it?

❷ ** Look at what two people will be doing tomorrow and complete the sentences using the Future Continuous.

You
9 a.m. get up
10 a.m. have breakfast
11 a.m. leave home
12 p.m. get to supermarket
3 p.m. have lunch
4.30 p.m. read the local paper

Me
8.45 start work
9.45–10.30 clean the tables in the restaurant
10.45–11.30 get the restaurant ready for lunch
12 p.m. open the restaurant
2.30–4.30 tidy the restaurant
4.30–5.15 walk home

1 When you get up, I'*ll be working.*
2 By the time you start your breakfast, _____
3 When you leave home, _____
4 By the time you get to the supermarket, _____
5 When you're having lunch, _____
6 While you're reading the local paper, _____

3 ** Complete the dialogues with the verbs below in the Future Continuous.

> do   drive   go   leave   listen   ~~play~~   watch

A: Do you want to come out with us on Friday evening?

B: I'm not sure. I ¹ _'ll be playing_ football in the afternoon. What time ² _____ you _____ out?

A: I ³_____ home at about 7 o'clock.

A: What ⁴_____ you at three o'clock tomorrow afternoon?

B: I don't know. Why?

A: We ⁵_____ past your house on our way to my aunt's. I can ask my dad to stop for a few minutes if you're not busy.

A: There's a good film on television this evening.

B: Well, I ⁶_____ it.

A: Why not?

B: I ⁷_____ to my new CD.

4 *** Put the verbs in brackets into the correct form. Use the Future Continuous where possible. Use the Future Simple where the Future Continuous is not possible.

A: What's this exciting news you've got?

B: I ¹_'ll tell_ (tell) you later.

A: ²_____ (your dad / work) late this evening?

B: Yes. He ³_____ (not come) home until about ten o'clock.

A: ⁴_____ (you / go) shopping this afternoon?

B: No, I ⁵_____ (not have) time.

A: ⁶_____ (you / cycle) to school tomorrow?

B: No, my parents ⁷_____ (not let) me. They say that there's too much traffic.

Grammar Alive Requests

5 Complete the requests using the Future Continuous and then complete the dialogues with the correct sentences (a–f).

1 A: you / open / that box of chocolates soon?
Will you be opening that box of chocolates soon?

B: I might, why?

A: _f_

2 A: you / go / downstairs?
_____

B: Yes, in a minute.

A: ___

3 A: you / do / your maths homework soon?
_____

B: Yes, why?

A: ___

4 A: you / go / to school by car tomorrow?
_____

B: Yes, my mum will be taking me.

A: ___

5 A: you / play / tennis tomorrow?
_____

B: Yes, with Nathan.

A: ___

6 A: you / watch / the football on TV tonight?
_____

B: No, we'll be watching the film.

A: ___

a Could you ask her if she'll take me too?

b Could you record it for me so I can watch it tomorrow?

c Could we do it together? I don't understand it.

d Can I come and watch you?

e Could you get me some fruit juice from the fridge?

f Can I have one when you do?

1 Order the words to make questions.

1 Which / rainforest / the / world / the / is / biggest / in
   Which is the biggest rainforest in the world?

2 many / butterfly / How / are / Europe / of / in / species / there
   _____

3 is / What / effect / water cycle / the
   _____

4 are / the / disappearing / rainforests / Why
   _____

2 2.10 Listen to the interview and answer the questions from exercise 1.

1 *The Amazon* _____

2 _____

3 _____
   _____

4 _____
   _____

3 2.10 Listen again. Complete the notes about rainforests.

1 How much rain falls in a rainforest?
   _____

2 How much of the surface of the Earth is rainforest?
   _____

3 How much of the world's oxygen is produced in the Amazon?
   _____

4 How many of the world's species of plants come from rainforests?
   _____

5 How many species are lost every day?
   _____

6 What can the local people in the rainforests help us to find?
   _____

7 How many different kinds of fruit do the local people eat in rainforests?
   _____

8 What is the main problem with cutting down rainforests for farming?
   _____

9 Why are rainforests disappearing in India?
   _____

Word Builder *take*

4 Complete the sentences with the words below.

action   advantage of   ~~break~~   care of   part in

1 You've been working hard all day. Take a
   break for a few hours.

2 When my mum was in hospital, my aunt took _____ me.

3 We've decided to take _____ to try to save the tiger from extinction.

4 Are you going to take _____ the sports day next week?

5 We should take _____ the cheap prices and buy some new clothes.

Sentence Builder Reduced relative clauses

5 Complete the second sentence so that it has the same meaning as the one above. Use the word in capitals.

1 People who live in rainforests know a lot about the plants there.
   (LIVING)
   People living in rainforests know a lot about the plants there.

2 Michelle Stevens, a radio presenter working on the *Earth Matters* programme, has just written a book.
   (WHO)
   Michelle Stevens, a radio presenter _____ *Earth Matters* programme, has just written a book.

3 Farmers who cut down rainforests are destroying the planet.
   (CUTTING)
   _____ rainforests are destroying the planet.

4 Everyone listening to Peter Jenkins agrees with what he says.
   (WHO)
   _____ to Peter Jenkins agrees with what he says.

LESSON **24** GRAMMAR
myself, yourself, ourselves, each other

❶ * **Choose the correct word to complete the sentences.**

1 My parents taught *ourselves*/*themselves* how to make a wind turbine.

2 Beyoncé *herself*/*yourself*, couldn't have sung the song better than I did.

3 My brother hurt *yourself*/*himself* while he was kite surfing.

4 I, *myself*/*ourselves*, always recycle plastic and paper.

5 Did you do all that work *itself*/*yourself*?

6 This rubbish won't recycle *itself*/*themselves*, you know.

7 We made *ourselves*/*themselves* something to eat.

8 The children made their breakfast *themselves*/*ourselves*.

9 My sister designed a website *itself*/*herself*.

❷ ** **Complete the sentences with the words below.**

> herself   himself   itself   ~~myself~~   ourselves
> themselves   yourself

1 I, _myself_ , have planted three trees this week.

2 I like this gadget. It switches _____ off if you don't use it for five minutes.

3 My dad bought _____ a book about the landscapes of Great Britain.

4 You've got a great computer. Now you need to get _____ some games to play on it.

5 Did your mum make this cake _____? It's delicious.

6 If we have our own company, we can pay _____ as much money as we want!

7 My uncle and aunt don't need anyone to help them in the home. They can do everything _____.

❸ ** **Complete the dialogues with the words in capitals. There is an extra word in each section.**

> ~~me~~   myself   you   yourself

A: Will you help [1] _me_ with this homework?

B: No. You have to do it [2] _____. That's what the teacher told [3] _____.

> me   myself   them   themselves

A: Mark and Steve were asking about the CDs that you borrowed.

B: Oh no. I forgot to bring [4] _____. They're at school.

A: Do you want [5] _____ to get them?

B: No, I'll get them [6] _____ later.

> ourself   himself   herself   you

A: Wow. You and Susan have tidied the house while we've been out.

B: Well, Susan did most of it [7] _____. I helped her a little. And we made dinner for [8] _____, too. Do you want some?

A: I'd love some but your dad bought [9] _____ a Chinese takeaway.

❹ *** **Complete the text with the correct object pronoun, reflexive pronoun or *each other*.**

Thank you Mr Davies and thank you, everyone, for choosing [1] _me_ to be the head student for this year. There have always been lots of good ideas from students about the school and I [2] _____ have a few ideas of my own.

We are lucky that we have such great teachers here. We know that they help [3] _____ a lot with our studies and personal problems and we are all very grateful to [4] _____ for that help. However, I believe that we, the students, should do more to help [5] _____ with homework and other problems. After all, we are the same age and understand [6] _____.

I also think that students in years twelve and thirteen should be allowed to decide for [7] _____ what to wear to school. They are old enough to know what not to wear. I know Mr Davies has suggested a similar idea in the past but that the parents disagreed with [8] _____. My question is, why do we ask the parents at all? Do we tell [9] _____ what they can wear? NO!

Workshop 4

Writing

1 Complete these formal expressions from a letter of complaint.

1 Dear _Sir/ Madam_
2 I am _____ to you about ...
3 I would be _____ if you could give me a full _____ of my money.
4 I look _____ to _____ from you.
5 Yours _____

2 Choose the correct cause linkers to complete the sentences.

1 _As_/Due to your brochure said that everything was included in the price, I didn't take much money.
2 I couldn't sleep _because of/because_ there was such a loud noise outside my room.
3 I was unable to go on any of the trips _as/because of_ illness.
4 The hotel you said we would stay at was closed _due to/ because_ repairs.
5 I was only able to eat _because/due to_ another guest agreed to lend me some money.

3 Look at the advert and the handwritten notes and complete the problems below.

> ### Landscape Tours
>
> A one week holiday seeing the very best landscapes of this country! Walk up hills, through beautiful valleys and forests and along quiet beaches and cliffs.
>
> * Easy walks for all ages. —→ *Not easy at all*
>
> * Helpful guides who can tell you all about the wildlife. —→ *They didn't know anything*
>
> * Stay in comfortable accommodation. —→ *Uncomfortable bed*
>
> * Travel in our luxury coach. —→ *Not a luxury — dirty toilets*
>
> * £350 a week for accommodation, food, travel and walks —→ *had to pay for lunch*

1 I was really tired after the walks because they _weren't easy at all_.
2 As _____, we didn't learn anything and the walks were boring.
3 I couldn't sleep well due to _____.
4 I didn't enjoy travelling on the coach because of _____.
5 As _____, I spent about one hundred pounds more than I expected.

4 Imagine you are the person who went on the Landscape Tour and wrote the notes on the advert. Write a letter of complaint. Write between 120 and 180 words.

Speaking

1 Choose the correct responses.

1 **A:** It's important to save energy.
   B: _Yes, it is_/Yes, I do.
2 **A:** I hate it when people drop litter.
   B: _Yes, I do./So do I._
3 **A:** I don't really understand climate change.
   B: _So do I./Neither do I._
4 **A:** I always cycle to school, even when it's raining.
   B: _I don't./I do._
5 **A:** I don't recycle.
   B: _I don't./I do._
6 **A:** Don't you think that there is too much traffic?
   B: _I think so too./Yes, I do._

2 **2.11** Complete the dialogues with the correct words. Then listen to check.

1 **A:** I believe that climate change is the biggest problem for the world.
   B: _So_ _do_ I.
2 **A:** The police should stop people from dropping litter. _____ you think so?
   B: Yes, I _____.
3 **A:** I think everyone should have to share their car. Don't you?
   B: No, I don't _____ _____. I don't think that's a _____ idea.
4 **A:** Solar panels are a really good thing, _____ _____?
   B: Yes, they _____.
5 **A:** I don't think there are enough cycle lanes.
   B: _____ _____ I.

Check Your Progress 8

1 My environment **Complete the words with the correct letters.**

1 The climate in very hot, rainy countries near the equator.
t _ _ p _ _ _ _   e _ _ _ t _ _ _ a _
2 The climate in countries like Italy and southern France. Hot dry summers and cool, wet winters.
M _ _ _ t _ _ _ _ n _ _ _
3 The climate in countries like England. Warm summers and cool winters with no big extremes.
t _ _ p _ _ _ t _
4 An area of low flat ground that is wet and soft
m _ _ _ _
5 A large area of flat dry land
p _ _ i _
6 An environmental problem
c _ _ _ _ _ e c _ _ _ _ e

/8

2 My environment **Complete the words to make four problems and four solutions.**

Problems
1 traffic j_ _ _ _ _ _ _ _ _ _
2 climate c_ _ _ _ _ _ _ _ _ _
3 e_ _ _ _ _ _ _ _ _ _ of species
4 exhaust f_ _ _ _ _ _
Solutions
5 Use r_ _ _ _ _ _ _ _ _ _ energy.
6 P _ _ _ _ _ _ _ trees.
7 S_ _ _ _ _ _ _ _ _ _ cars.
8 Use p_ _ _ _ _ _ _ _ _ _ transport.

/8

3 Expressions with *take* **Complete the sentences with the correct word.**

1 Let's _ _ _ _ _ _ _ _ _ _ _ a break and have a drink. We can do some more work later.
2 We must do more to take _ _ _ _ _ _ _ _ _ _ _ of the environment.
3 We decided to take some _ _ _ _ _ _ _ _ _ _ _and plant trees in our local park.
4 I haven't got time to take _ _ _ _ _ _ _ _ _ _ _ in any more activities.
5 Don't complain about the snow. Let's take _ _ _ _ _ _ _ _ _ _ _ of it and go skiing.

/5

4 Future Continuous **Look at the plans and complete the questions and replies using the Future Continuous.**

10–12 English test
12–1 lunch – go to the pizzeria with Craig.

1 What / you / do tomorrow at 11 a.m.?
_____
I / do / an English test.
_____
2 you / eat / lunch at school?
_____
No I won't. Craig and I / go / to the pizzeria.
_____

/4

5 *myself, yourself, ourselves* and *each other* **Complete the sentences with the correct reflexive pronoun or *each other*.**

1 Stop looking at _ _ _ _ _ _ _ _ _ _ _ in the mirror. We're late.
2 I sometimes talk to _ _ _ _ _ _ _ _ _ _ _ when I'm walking along the street.
3 Mum's bought _ _ _ _ _ _ _ _ _ _ _ a new dress.
4 My girlfriend and I are going to email _ _ _ _ _ _ _ _ _ _ _ every day while she is on holiday.
5 Jo and I painted our bedrooms _ _ _ _ _ _ _ _ _ _ _.

/5

TOTAL SCORE /30

Module Diary

1 **Look at the objectives on page 61 in the Students' Book. Choose three and evaluate your learning.**

1 Now I can _____
well / quite well / with problems.
2 Now I can _____
well / quite well / with problems.
3 Now I can _____
well / quite well / with problems

2 **Look at your results. What language areas in this module do you need to study more?**

Exam Choice 4

Reading

1 Read the text quickly and complete the sentences with one or two words in each gap. For each sentence, say whether it is a fact (F) or opinion (O).

1 The building is _perfect for_ for the activities you can do there. _O_

2 The car park is _____ if you use the centre. ___

3 The centre is not _____ yet. ___

4 The equipment is _____ regularly. ___

5 A month ticket costs £25, which is very good _____. ___

6 You can do indoor activities _____ hours a day. ___

2 Read the text again. Match the questions (a-i) with the gaps (1-8) in the text. There is one extra question.

a How safe is it?

b Do you have to be a member?

c Do I have to book a place in advance?

d How much does it cost?

e Is it worth the money?

f Do they have qualified instructors?

g Where is it?

h What's the best time to go?

i What can I do there?

THE NEW ACTIVITY CENTRE

YOUR QUESTIONS ANSWERED ...

1 ___ The centre opened in the old theatre near the beach. There have been a lot of changes to the building and it is now perfect for the activities you can do there. There is also a big car park outside which costs £10 but is free if you are using the activity centre.

2 ___ At the moment, the centre is not finished so the number of activities offered is still quite small. There are climbing walls as well as lots of indoor sports available. The centre also organises kite surfing, kayaking and surfing on the beach. Indoor skiing will be possible next year.

3 ___ The centre is part of a group of activity centres. They first opened in America twenty-five years ago and they are proud that, in all that time, there has never been a serious accident. The activities are very well organised and the equipment is checked regularly.

4 ___ There are a number of different tickets available. You can pay for one hour, half a day or one day or you can buy a weekly, monthly or yearly ticket. One hour is quite expensive at £5 but a monthly ticket is only £25, which is very good value.

5 ___ As we said above, this depends on the kind of ticket you buy. The one hour ticket is not a very good choice as you may spend a lot of the time waiting to do an activity, especially when the centre is busy. If you buy a monthly or yearly ticket and use the centre a lot, it's one of the best bargains you can find.

6 ___ At the moment, it is impossible to book a place but this may change if the centre becomes very popular. So, just turn up and pay your money or show your ticket but, remember, if it is full, you might have to wait.

7 ___ There are two different kinds of workers at the centre. Those in orange shirts are generally students helping out in their free time. However, everyone wearing blue shirts must be trained in the sport that they are teaching and also know what to do in case of accidents or injuries.

8 ___ All indoor activities are available twenty-four hours a day, seven days a week although the outdoor events obviously aren't. We have been there during the week and at weekends. Mornings are quiet and Saturday afternoons are the most crowded. There can be queues from 6–8 p.m. during the week and from 2–8 p.m. on Saturdays and Sundays.

Listening

3 **2.12** Listen to an interview about a forest and complete the notes.

Epping Forest

1 Where is it? _____

2 How big is it? _____

3 When did it become a royal forest?
_____

4 Who has taken care of it since 1878?
_____

5 What species live in 'dead wood'?
_____

6 What examples of larger animals does the speaker mention? _____

7 Where do muntjacs come from?
_____

8 Name two problems the forest has.
_____

9 When does the special walk take place?
_____

Speaking

4 **2.13** Look at the visual materials and listen to two students discussing the questions. Complete their answers with the words below. There are three extra words.

New rules for rubbish to reduce waste

	Switzerland	Austria	Germany	UK
Recycling rates	52%	49.7%	48%	16%

agree   are   do (x 2)   don't   is   it   neither   so   there
think   too

Examiner: What issues does the material deal with?

A: I think the material deals with the problems of waste and how we can reduce this by recycling. Don't you
¹_____?

B: Yes, I ²_____. We can see some rubbish bins in the picture. The headline shows what the government is doing to solve the problem and the table shows that the UK has a bigger problem than a lot of other countries.

Examiner: What problems are caused by waste?

B: There are several problems, aren't ³_____ ?

A: Yes, there ⁴_____. There's litter in the streets, the problem of where to put rubbish and the fact that recycling can save energy and trees.

Examiner: How can we encourage people to recycle more?

A: It's a difficult problem, isn't ⁵_____?

B: Yes, it is. I don't think there are enough recycling bins.

A: ⁶_____ do I. People don't like carrying their rubbish a long way. But I don't like ideas like making people pay more to throw away their rubbish.

B: I ⁷_____. I ⁸_____ it's a very good idea.

Examiner: How much do you recycle?

A: I recycle paper, glass and plastic but I should recycle more.

B: Me ⁹_____. I know it's important but, sometimes, I'm lazy.

Exam Choice 4

Use of English

5 Complete the blog with the correct words.

June 10

I've booked my working holiday. It starts on 15 July and is for three weeks in Africa. I can't believe it. I've always been interested ¹_____ Africa and now I'm going to see it.

July 16

I'm here. It was a long journey - eight hours on a plane with my laptop. I'm glad I'm here because I'm bored ²_____ playing computer games now! I was a bit worried ³_____ finding my group at the airport but they were very well organised.

July 17

We had a long drive today to look for animals. We were on a big, flat, dry plain with a few bushes and trees in it. I thought the climate would be equatorial with lots of rain but it's more like semi-desert. Everything is very dry. Tomorrow, we're ⁴_____ to do something really exciting! We don't know what it is yet …

July 18

Our last rest day before we start working and what a day! We went sky ⁵_____ It was amazing. I've never taken ⁶_____ in anything as fun or as frightening as that before. That's it for the fun. Tomorrow, we'll ⁷_____ doing some work. I'm looking forward to it.

July 19

We started helping out at a local village. The people here want to use renewable energy but they can't do it all ⁸_____ so we're here to help them. We're going ⁹_____ build a wind turbine. At the same time, they're going to teach us about the animals and plants here so we're going to learn from each ¹⁰_____ . That's why this holiday is such a good idea.

Writing

6 Complete the email with the verbs *do, finish, go* and *send* in the gaps in the correct form. One verb is used twice.

Hi Rory,

Thanks for ¹_____ me the email. The activity centre sounds great but I'm going to look at their website before ²_____ there.

I really need to get some exercise and have some fun. For the last month, I've been studying for exams. That's four weeks without ³_____ anything except sitting in my room with my books. After ⁴_____ my last exam, I went out with some friends to an Italian restaurant. It was great to have time to talk to people again.

I must go now. Stella is coming in a minute. She's interested in ⁵_____ some exciting activities, too.

See you soon.

Katie.

7 Read the instructions below. Write an email.

- Someone has written to you. In your introduction, thank them for their email and make a short comment.
- In the main body of the email, tell your friend your news.
- Finish the email and give a reason why you have to stop writing.

Write between 80 and 120 words.

TOPIC TALK – VOCABULARY

1 **Complete the people's favourite subjects.**

1 Joe likes acting: d*rama*
2 Samantha loves drawing and painting:
   a_____ and d_____
3 Ed loves computers: i_____ and
   c_____ t_____
4 Lucy loves reading classic novels: E_____
   l_____
5 Neil likes learning about different religions:
   r_____ e_____
6 Mary likes discussing ideas: p_____
7 Paul enjoys learning about the world:
   g_____
8 Annie loves grammar: E_____ l_____

2 **Complete the text with the words below.**

analysing   concentrate   ~~memorising~~   online
organising   passing   present   solving   teams

Report card

Johnny Fisher. C+

Johnny is very good at [1] *_memorising_ facts
so he has no problem in* [2] *_____
exams. However, his classwork could be
better. He finds it difficult to* [3] *_____
in class and he doesn't work well in
* [4] *_____ because he doesn't listen
to anyone else. At home, he enjoys
working* [5] *_____ and he is very
good at* [6] *_____ information and
* [7] *_____ problems. Unfortunately, he
doesn't* [8] *_____ his work neatly so
he loses marks. He also needs to think about
* [9] *_____ his learning so that he has
time to finish everything without hurrying.*

3 **Read the information and write the extra-curricular activities in the correct places. There are three extra activities.**

adventure activities   astronomy   carpentry   chess
choir   dancing   ~~debating club~~   first aid   personal finance
orchestra   poetry club   the school magazine   voluntary work

At school, I do several different things apart from normal
lessons. I belong to a club where we discuss our opinions
and try to win the argument [1](*debating club*), a group of
musicians who play classical music [2](_____) and a
group of singers. [3](_____)
I do a board game for two people played on a black and
white board [4](_____), a physical activity where we
move to music [5](_____) and things to help people
who need help, such as old people. [6](_____)
I learn about how to help people who are hurt
[7](_____), how to make things from wood
[8](_____) and how to spend and save money carefully.
[9](_____)
I write for a publication full of news and articles written by
students. [10](_____)

4 **Complete the text with the correct words.**

The [1]s*ubject* I like best at school is drama and my
[2]l_____ favourite subject is maths. I'd like to
[3]d_____ it and do another language [4]i_____.
I suppose I'm good at English and languages but [5]n_____
[6]s_____ good at maths and sciences.
[7]O_____ class, I [8]b_____ to the film club and I
[9]d_____ adventure activities. It'd [10]b_____ great to
play football for the school team.

5 **Complete the profile so that it is true for you.**

1 Favourite school subject: _____
2 Least favourite school subject: _____
3 Learning skills I am good at: _____
4 Learning skills I am not so good at: _____
5 Extra-curricular activities I do: _____
6 Extra-curricular activities I'd like to do: _____

Would you like to live at school?

Harry Potter loved going to Hogwarts because it meant that he didn't have to live with his uncle and aunt but what do real school students think about the idea of living at school and only seeing their parents in the holidays?

1 _d_ I've never studied at a school where you eat, sleep and live. I'm sure there are some good things about them. For example, I think students there are probably more independent and the friendships they make would also probably be very strong. However, I'm not sure I'd like to go to a school like that. At my school, students leave school at 3 p.m. and are free to do what they like and go where they like. I guess there are good and bad things about each.

2 ___ When I was eleven, my parents decided I should live at school because they were going abroad to work. I hated it at first and I wrote to them every day. I wanted to be with them and didn't make any friends for a long time. When I left school, I said to myself that I would never send my own children to a school like that. Now, my oldest son is eleven and he's just started at my old school. The education you get is so much better than in the local schools here.

3 ___ My parents aren't rich enough to send me away to an expensive school which costs thousands of pounds a year. I'm very pleased about that. In my opinion, a child should grow up with his or her parents. You make friends with people who live near you and spend your free time in the real world. It's not right to spend your whole life with teachers watching you and telling you what to do. No one should have to do that!

4 ___ I nearly had to go away to school when I left primary school. I'm glad I didn't. Children of that age need things like their toys and family. Now I'm sixteen and one of my friends has just gone away to school. He was quite excited about it because he has had a few problems with his parents. I still wouldn't want to go, that's just my personality, but I can see that they might be quite a good idea for sixteen to eighteen year olds.

5 ___ I don't know anyone who lives at school. I'm very happy at my school but I think it would be quite fun. Some people say the teachers are always watching you but I don't think that's really true. You get free time and you make really good friends. I think it'd be great to have the chance to go to a school like that. I know I never will but it's nice to dream.

1 Read the text on the left and match the points of view (a–f) with the posts (1–5) in the magazine. There is one extra point of view.

a thinks such schools are good but too expensive.

b thinks that living at school can be a good thing but only for older students.

c would like to try living at school.

d can see advantages and disadvantages with living at school.

e changed his/her mind about living at school.

f doesn't think anyone should have to live at school.

2 Read the texts again. Do these sentences refer to normal schools (N) or schools where students live all the time (L)?

1 The students are more independent. _L_

2 The friendships are very strong. ___

3 Students are free to do what they want after school. ___

4 The education students get is better. ___

5 They are expensive. ___

6 You make friends with people who live near you. ___

7 You spend your free time in the 'real' world. ___

Word Builder Making nouns

3 Complete the sentences with the correct form of the words in capitals.

1 Our school football team are playing in the final of the London Schools' _championship_. CHAMPION

2 That was a great _____ by Heidi in the school play, wasn't it? PERFORM

3 Your _____ is very important which is why we are sending you to a different school. EDUCATE

4 Paul has the _____ but needs to work harder if he wants to pass his exams. ABLE

5 What's the main _____ between your new school and your old one? DIFFERENT

6 Mike's _____ is due to his friendly _____ and good looks. POPULAR/PERSON

7 Can you describe the man's _____? APPEAR

8 We need more _____ between the students and teachers at our school. COOPERATE

Sentence Builder Example linkers

4 Complete the sentences with *as, example, for, like* and *such*. You can use one word twice.

1 I do a lot of sports, _like_ football, basketball and running.

2 My friends and I go to lots of places in the evening, such _____ the cinema, the pizzeria and the sports centre.

3 I want to go to the best school, _____ my dad.

4 We read books by all the great writers in English Literature. For _____, Shakespeare, Dickens and Charlotte Bronte.

5 There are lots of good things about our school, _____ as the extra-curricular activities and the computer room.

6 Our teachers help us to be more independent. _____ example, we have to organise our own learning and analyse our progress.

Writing

5 Complete the sentences with your own ideas.

1 There are advantages to living at school, for

_____

_____

_____

2 There are a number of things which make one school better than the other, such _____

_____

_____

3 We should be able to learn about other things at school, like _____

_____

_____

4 I would / wouldn't like to live at school because

_____

_____

_____

26

Reported statements

REMEMBER

Complete exercises A-B before you start this lesson.

A Complete the sentences with the verb in brackets in the infinitive with *to*. Make the sentences positive (+) or negative (-).

1 Our French teacher told us _to memorise_ (memorise) twenty verbs for a test. (+)

2 The leader of the school orchestra asked me _not to sing_ (sing) so loudly. (-)

3 My English teacher advised me _____ (do) some extra-curricular activities. (+)

4 My parents advised me _____ (organise) my learning better. (+)

5 The doctor told me _____ (do) any sports for a month. (-)

6 My friend asked me _____ (teach) him how to cook. (+)

7 All my friends advised me _____ (drop) French in Year nine. (-)

8 I told my friend _____ (worry) so much about her exams. (-)

B Change the direct speech into reported orders, requests and advice.

1 (My female friend to me): Could you help me with my English literature homework, please?
My friend asked me to help her with her
English literature homework.

2 (My mum to me): Don't eat so quickly!
_____
_____

3 (My friend to me): You should join the debating club.
_____
_____

4 (My male friend to me): Please don't forget to bring my CDs to school.
_____
_____

5 (Our teacher to all of us): Concentrate!
_____
_____

6 (Me to my younger brother): You shouldn't spend so much time on the internet.
_____
_____

1 * Match the speakers with what they said. Two speakers match the same reported statement.

1 **Maria:** _e_ | I will organise my learning.

2 **Adam:** ___ | I have organised my learning.

3 **Samantha:** ___ | I organised my learning.

4 **Natalie:** ___ | I am organising my learning.

5 **Noel:** ___ | I can organise my learning.

6 **Phil:** ___ | I organise my learning.

He/She said that he/she:

a could organise his/her learning.
b had organised his/her learning.
c was organising his/her learning.
d organised his/her learning.
e would organise his/her learning.

2 ** Choose the correct words to complete the sentences.

1 'I passed all my exams,' said Tom.
Tom said that he *has passed/had passed* all his exams.

2 'I've decided to do some charity work,' said Sue.
Sue said that she *decided/had decided* to do some charity work.

3 'I don't like working in teams,' said Frank.
Frank said that he *didn't like/hadn't liked* working in teams.

4 'You can drop one subject in Year twelve,' our teacher told us.
Our teacher told us that we *would/could* drop one subject in Year twelve.

5 'Your article will be on the front cover of the school magazine,' Mr Roberts said.
Mr Roberts said that *your/my* article would be on the front cover of the school magazine.

6 'You are working very hard,' my mum told me.
My mum told me that I *have been working/was working* very hard.

7 'I can't memorise numbers,' said Craig.
Craig said that *I/he* couldn't memorise numbers.

3 ** Complete the sentences with a verb in the correct form.

1 Harry said that he could solve our problems.
'I ___can___ solve your problems,' said Harry.

2 Tina said that she was waiting for Stuart.
'I _____ for Stuart,' said Tina.

3 Melanie said that she hadn't had her exam results yet.
'I _____ my exam results yet,' said Melanie.

4 Chris said that he would meet us in the pizzeria.
'I _____ you in the pizzeria,' said Chris.

5 Liam said that he often went to the school's film club.
'I often _____ to the school's film club,' said Liam.

6 Aaron said that he had failed two exams in Year ten but that he hadn't failed any exams in Year eleven yet.
'I _____ two exams in Year ten but I _____ any exams in Year eleven yet.'

4 *** Look at the report and complete the text with correct form of the verbs in brackets.

> School report – Lucy Jones
> Position in class: Fifteenth
> Homework done: 12/25
> Behaviour: Noisy, doesn't concentrate
> Tests: English 56%
>   Geography 61%
>   Music 18%
>   IT 90%
>   French 15%
>   Maths No result – talking
>   in the exam.
>
> Teacher's comments:
> Lucy spends her time playing on her mobile phone and talking. She must work harder next year. I am going to talk to her before the end of term to discuss her future.

Mum: Oh Lucy, look at this report. You said you ¹ ___were___ (be) the best student in your class but you aren't. You also told us that you always ² _____ (do) your homework but you've done less than half this year. You told us that you ³ _____ (try) to be a good student and that you always ⁴ _____ (work) hard. And look at your exam results. You told us that you ⁵ _____ (pass) your music exam. That wasn't true, was it? And you said that you ⁶ _____ (can) speak French really well. And what about maths? You didn't tell us that you ⁷ _____ (not finish) your test. And what's this at the bottom? Your teacher said he ⁸ _____ (talk) to you about your future? Did he? What did he say?

Grammar Alive Reporting (1)

5 Read what Claire says and then complete the reported form.

> I'm in Year ten. I like English literature. My class are reading *Romeo and Juliet*. It's my favourite story. We haven't finished it yet but I know what happens at the end because I've seen the film.

Claire said that ¹ _she was_ in Year ten at school and that ² _____ English literature. She then told us that ³ _____ *Romeo and Juliet* which she said ⁴ _____ favourite story. She told us that ⁵ _____ it yet but that ⁶ _____ what ⁷ _____ at the end because ⁸ _____ the film.

1 Match the beginnings of the rules (1-5) with the correct endings (a-e).

You have to:

1 arrive _b_
2 attend ___
3 hand in ___
4 leave ___
5 wear ___

a your homework on time.
b on time.
c personal items at home.
d a uniform.
e school daily.

2 Put the words below in the correct part of the table.

aggressive behaviour ~~assembly hall~~ bullying
competitive fighting gym high-speed internet
projectors science labs sociable strict wi-fi

Facilities	Atmosphere	Equipment	Problems
assembly hall			

Talk Builder Asking for permission

3 〔2.14〕 Complete an informal dialogue with the correct phrases below. Then listen to check.

Hey, Is it okay if I want to speak to Look, I've got to go
No way Oh, all right See you

William: ¹ _Hey,_ Jake!
Jake: Yes?
William: ² _____ you.
Jake: What about?
William: ³ _____ I go to lunch with you?
Jake: Yes, okay, if you pay!
William: ⁴ _____ !
Jake: Well, can you lend me some money until tomorrow?
William: ⁵ _____ . But don't forget.
Jake: Thanks, I won't.
...
Jake: That was a good pizza.
William: Yes, it was. ⁶ _____ . I've got chess club.
Jake: Okay, bye.
William: ⁷ _____

4 〔2.15〕 Listen to the beginning and ending of a conversation between a school student and a teacher. Choose the correct answers to complete the conversation. Then listen to check.

Jamie: ¹(Excuse me)/Hey, Miss Lane. ²*I want to speak to you/Could I possibly have a word with you, please?*
Miss Lane: ³*I'm sorry but I'm busy./No way.*
Jamie: It won't take a minute, miss.
...
Jamie: Erm... if I bring you the guidebook on Monday, is it okay if I take a bit longer on my homework?
Miss Lane: How much longer?
Jamie ⁴*Can I/Would it be all right if* I hand it in a week late? You know, when you get back from your holiday in Paris?
Miss Lane: Yes, you can do that.
Jamie: Great! ⁵*I'm sorry but I really must be going./Look, I've got to go.* I've got football practice again.
Miss Lane: Goodbye, Jamie. See you on Monday. And good luck in the match.
Jamie: Thanks. ⁶*Goodbye!/See you!*

5 〔2.16〕 Listen to a second conversation between the school student and a friend. Complete the conversation with the correct words.

Jamie: ¹ _Hey_ , Katie! I want to ² _____ to you.
Katie: What Jamie? I'm in a real hurry.
Jamie: ³ _____ I borrow your guide book of Paris? The one you lent me last summer.
Katie: ⁴ _____ , Jamie, I'm really busy. Can't you buy one?
Jamie: Oh come on, Katie. Can't I come round and pick it up? I can come on Saturday evening, early.
Katie: We'll all be out. Sorry, Jamie.
Jamie: Well, what about Sunday? Sunday morning.
Katie: Oh, ⁵ _____ right. At about ten. ⁶ _____ , I've really got to go. I've got my dance class in five minutes.
Jamie: Okay, thanks Katie. By the way, are you coming to the match on Saturday?
Katie: Maybe, if I've got time. ⁷ _____ you.
Jamie: Right, see you on Sunday at ten. Don't forget.
Katie: I won't. Bye. See you Jamie.

Check Your Progress 9

1 School (1) **Choose the correct words to complete the sentences.**

1 We're studying Charles Dickens in English *studies/ literature/education* at the moment.
2 My teacher told my parents that I have trouble *concentrating/analysing/presenting* in class.
3 Excuse me. What is ICT? It's information and computer *training/teaching/technology*.
4 I'm not very good at *memorising/organising/solving facts*.
5 I'd like to do business *education/design/studies* at university.
6 We're learning how to *solve/assess/concentrate* our progress.

/6

2 School (1) **Complete the sentences with the correct form of *do, belong, write* or *learn*.**

Last year, I ¹_____ for the school magazine and I ²_____ some voluntary work. This year, I ³_____ to the debating club.
At my school, we ⁴_____ about useful things like first aid and life saving. We can also ⁵_____ adventure activities. It's great.
I've already ⁶_____ three things for the school magazine.

/6

3 Making nouns **Complete the sentences with the correct form of the words below. There is one extra word.**

able   appear   differ   educate   embarrass   evident
friend

1 Are there any _____ between ICT and technology?
2 I hope our _____ will last even if we go to different universities.
3 There is no real _____ that boys do better in science and maths than girls.
4 I went bright red with _____ when I realised I was wearing one black shoe and one brown one.
5 Tom's _____ is quite strange, especially his hair, but he's very nice.
6 Dan's got an amazing _____ to memorise facts.

/6

4 Reported statements **Complete the second sentence so that it has the same meaning as the one above.**

1 'I never drink coffee before exams,' said Oliver.
Oliver said that _____ before exams.
2 Tom told us that he wanted to join the orchestra.
'_____ the school orchestra,' said Tom.
3 'A chess club has opened,' said my teacher.
The headmaster said that _____.
4 Marianna said that she was learning Italian.
'_____ Italian,' said Marianna.
5 Jack's parents told him that he would have to work harder.
'_____ work harder,' said Jack's parents.
6 Angie's brother told her that she could borrow his laptop.
'_____ laptop,' Angie's brother told her.

/6

5 Asking for permission **Complete sentences with the correct words.**

A: ¹E_____ me, Mr Finch, could I possibly have a ²w_____ with you, please?
B: Yes, what do you want, Charlie?
A: ³W_____ it be okay if I missed PE today?
B: I'm ⁴s_____ but all students have to do PE.
A: Could I go to the nurse and see what she says?
B: Yes, you can do that. Now, I'm sorry but I ⁵r_____ ⁶m_____ be going.

/6

TOTAL SCORE   */30*

Module Diary

1 Look at the objectives on page 69 in the Students' Book. Choose three and evaluate your learning.

1 Now I can _____
well / quite well / with problems.
2 Now I can _____
well / quite well / with problems.
3 Now I can _____
well / quite well / with problems.

2 Look at your results. What language areas in this module do you need to study more?

Sound Choice 5

Sound Check

Say the words and expressions below.

a think, this, basic, vision (Exercise 1)

b later, area, turbine (Exercises 2 and 3)

c change, share, think, physical (Exercise 4)

d Don't you think so? Can I borrow your CD? (Exercise 5)

e exam, examination, personal, personality (Exercise 6)

2.17 **Listen and check your answers. Which sounds and expressions did you have problems with? Choose three exercises to do below.**

1 **2.18** **Consonants - /s/, /ʒ/, /ð/ and /θ/ Put the words below in the correct category. Then listen and repeat them.**

weather   occasionally   theatre   aggressive
comprehensive   neither   enthusiastic   decision

/s/	/ʒ/	/ð/	/θ/
basic	vision	this	think
aggressive			

2 **2.19** **Vowels - /ə/ Listen and repeat the schwa sound /ə/. Repeat the words below making sure the underlined letters are said with the schwa sound.**

1 later   **3** area   **5** literature

2 never   **4** drama   **6** serious

3 **2.20** **Vowels - /ɜː/ Listen to three words which have the /ɜː/ sound. Then tick (✓) the word in each pair that also has the same sound. Then listen to check.**

bird   heard   murder

1 turbine ✓   sure ☐

2 pour ☐   journey ☐

3 serious ☐   expert ☐

4 work ☐   perform ☐

5 beard ☐   learn ☐

4 **2.21** **Spelling Listen and repeat the words below. Then listen again and write them in the correct place in the table. One word contains both *ch* and *sh*.**

change   think   share   philosophy   sixth   atmosphere
chat   marsh   thousand   physical   championship

sh	ch	th	ph
push	church	the	photo
	change		

5 **2.22** **Expressions - intonation Listen to the expressions and repeat them with the same intonation.**

1 Don't you think so?

2 Don't you want to?

3 Don't you agree?

4 Don't you?

5 Could I have a word with you, please?

6 Would it be all right if I arrived late?

7 Can I borrow your CD?

6 **2.23** **Difficult words - shifting stress Look at the groups of words and underline where the main stress is. Does the stress change when the word changes form or not? Listen to check and repeat the words.**

Noun formed with: - *ship*

friend - friendship	champion - championship

Noun formed with: -*tion*

exam - examination	educate - education	cooperate - cooperation

Noun formed with: -*ment*

develop - development	embarrass - embarrassment	arrange - arrangement

Noun formed with: -*ence* / -*ance*

appear - appearance	perform - performance	different - difference

Noun formed with: -*ity*

able - ability	popular - popularity	personal - personality

MODULE 10 CAREERS

TOPIC TALK – VOCABULARY

1 Label the career areas in the pictures.

1 t*ourism*

2 c_____

3 the m_____

4 s_____ b_____

5 f_____

6 m_____

2 Match the sentences (1-8) with the jobs (a-h).

1 He makes me laugh. _d_
2 She's got a hundred cows. ___
3 He writes for a local newspaper. ___
4 He'll look at your car for you. ___
5 She'll arrest the burglars. ___
6 She'll stop them sending you to prison. ___
7 He works in a hospital and makes people better. ___
8 She'll talk to you and try to make you understand your problems. ___

a mechanic
b psychotherapist
c surgeon
d comedian
e police officer
f farmer
g lawyer
h journalist

3 Complete the words with the correct letters. Use the clues in brackets to help you.

1 Good at: c o m mu n i c a t i n g ideas (telling other people your ideas)
  Best job: p _ _ _ t _ c _ (working in the government)
2 Good at: d _ _ l _ _ _ with m _ _ e _ (knowing how much to spend and save)
  Best job: f _ _ _ n _ _ (a job involving money)
3 Good at: doing e _ _ _ r _ m _ _ _ _ (working in a laboratory and trying new things)
  Best job: s _ _ e _ c _ (chemistry, physics, biology)
4 Good at: r _ p _ _ r _ _ _ things (taking broken things and making them work again)
  Best job: e _ g _ _ _ _ r _ _ _ (working with machines and building things)
5 Good at: d _ _ l _ _ _ with people (helping, talking to and managing people)
  Best job: e _ _ c _ _ _ o _ (teaching or training)

4 Complete the conversation with the words below. There are four extra words.

business calculations career dealing engineering future ~~no~~ office part-time pretty summer

A: I'd like some careers advice but I've got [1] _no_ idea about what I want to do in the future.
B: I see. Tell me about yourself.
A: Well, I'm [2]_____ good at maths and doing [3]_____.
B: Well, they are very useful abilities. There are lots of jobs you could do.
A: But I don't want to work in a bank or an [4]_____. I think I'd enjoy a [5]_____ in the media.
B: I see. Well, you should try to get a [6]_____ job with a local newspaper. I know some people who work there. Maybe I can help you. Have you ever worked for a newspaper before?
A: No. I've done [7]_____ work but only in restaurants and I've worked in a shop on Saturday mornings.
B: Well, it's good that you've had some experience.

83

28

GRAMMAR
Reported questions

REMEMBER

Complete exercises A–B before you start lesson 30, page 87.

Ⓐ Match the beginnings to the correct endings to make Present or Future Conditional sentences.

1 If it snows _b_	**a** if you get money for your birthday?
2 If it snows tomorrow ___	**b** there are always lots of accidents.
3 If a boy goes to an all boys school ___	**c** he usually concentrates better.
4 If my brother goes to an all boys school ___	**d** he will concentrate better.
5 If students do too many extra-curricular activities ___	**e** they won't have enough time for their studies.
6 If my friends do too many extra-curricular activities this year ___	**f** they often don't have enough time for their studies.
7 Will you get a new computer ___	**g** if your parents give you some money for passing these exams?
8 Do you spend everything immediately ___	**h** I'll go to school by bus.

Ⓑ Complete the sentences with the correct form of the Present or Future Conditional.

1 If you feel tired this evening, _will you go_ (you / go) to bed early?

2 In the summer, we always go to the lake if it _____ (be) sunny.

3 If I'm busy with exams or things, I often _____ (not send) emails or texts for days.

4 I _____ (not write) for the school magazine next year if I have too much work to do.

5 If the school starts an astronomy club next year, _____ (you / join) it?

6 _____ (the students in your class work) harder if your teachers shout?

7 My parents will be upset if I _____ (not pass) these exams.

8 If my sister is sad, she always _____ (listen) to sad songs on her MP3 player.

❶ * What did the person actually say when replying to the questions?

1 My friend asked me where my dad worked.
   ⓐ He works in a garage.
   b He worked in a garage.

2 My mum asked me when I would do the washing up.
   a I'd do it later.
   b I'll do it later.

3 John's friend asked him how many times he had been to America.
   a I'd never been there.
   b I've never been there.

4 Jane's mum asked her where she had been.
   a I'd been to the cinema.
   b I've been to the cinema.

5 Chris asked us where we were working.
   a We're working in a café by the beach.
   b We were working in a café by the beach.

6 My cousin asked me if I could swim.
   a Yes, I could.
   b Yes, I can.

❷ * Choose the correct answer to complete the sentences.

1 What is your job?
   He asked me what *was my job/my job was.*

2 What do you want to do in the future?
   She asked me what *I wanted to do/do I want to do* in the future.

3 Are your parents teachers?
   She asked me *were my parents teachers/if my parents were teachers.*

4 Does your mum work in an office?
   He asked me *did my mum work/if my mum worked* in an office.

5 Will you work as a waiter again?
   I asked my friend *would he work/if he would work* as a waiter again.

6 How many summer jobs have you had?
   They asked me how many summer jobs *I had had/had I had.*

7 When are you going to Italy?
   She asked me *when was I/when I was* going to Italy.

8 Did you go to the football match?
   He asked me if *had I gone/I had gone* to the football match.

3 ** Complete the reported questions.

1 What does your father do?
He asked me what _my father did_.

2 Can you repair cars?
I asked the man _____ repair cars.

3 Do you want to work in the media?
My teacher asked me _____ to work in the media.

4 What's your uniform like?
My friend asked me what _____ like.

5 Are you thinking of getting a new job?
My boss asked me _____ of getting a new job.

6 Where did you work in the holidays?
I asked my girlfriend where _____ in the holidays.

7 When will we get our money?
We asked our boss when _____ our money.

8 Where does your mum work?
Paul asked me where _____.

4 *** Complete the conversation with the reported form of the questions in brackets. In two answers, you don't have to change the tense of the verb.

A: I don't think I'm going to keep my summer job for very long.

B: Why not?

A: I had an interview with my boss today. At first she was quite friendly. She asked
[1] _if I was enjoying my job_ (Are you enjoying your job?) and [2] _____ (Is there anything you need?).

B: She sounds nice.

A: That's what I thought. I relaxed, which was a mistake. Then she asked [3] _____ (Do you know what time we start work?). I said 'Yes' and she asked [4] _____ (How many times have you been late since you started work?).

B: What did you say?

A: Nothing. So she looked at me and asked
[5] _____ (Did you hear what I said?). I told her I had and asked her [6] _____ (Will I lose my job?). She said she would tell me tomorrow. I've got another meeting at ten o'clock.

B: Why does she want another meeting?

A: She wants to know [7] _____ (Do I really want the job?) and [8] _____ (How will I change?). I don't know the answer to either question!

Grammar Alive Reporting (2)

5 Look at the conversation between a journalist and a comedian and then complete the report.

Journalist: Do you enjoy being a comedian?
Jake: Sometimes. I like it when I'm working.
Journalist: What's wrong with it at other times?
Jake: People think I should be funny all the time.
Journalist: Do they ask you to tell jokes?
Jake: All the time. I hate it.
Journalist: Can you tell me a joke?
Jake: No.
Journalist: What are you doing now?
Jake: I'm making a television show.
Journalist: When will it be on television?
Jake: In December.

I asked Jake [1] _if he enjoyed being a comedian_ and he said that he liked it when he was working. I then [2] _____ at other times and he said that people thought he should be funny all the time. I [3] _____ to tell jokes and he said that they did, all the time, and that he hated it so I [4] _____ but he said 'No'. I think he knew I was joking. I didn't have much time so I [5] _____. He told me he was making a television show so I finished the interview by asking [6] _____ and he said that it would be on in December.

1 **2.24** Listen to an interview between a manager and a part-time employee and answer the questions.

1 Is she just starting or just finishing work?

_____

2 Does the manager give her some ideas or does she give the manager some ideas?

_____

3 How many ideas are discussed?

_____

2 **2.24** Listen again and choose the correct answers.

1 Which sentence is true about the work Alison has done?
  a She did the same thing every day.
  b She only did things she wanted to do.
  c She did different things, some of which she wanted to do.

2 At the moment, the centre doesn't:
  a have any activities for children.
  b allow parents to leave their children with other people to look after them.
  c allow families with children to come to the centre.

3 Alison thinks that:
  a she could work with children now.
  b she should find somewhere to do a first aid course.
  c the centre should train the people who work with children in first aid.

4 Alison gets on well with:
  a all the other part-time workers.
  b everyone who works at the centre.
  c some of the part-time workers and some of the full-time workers.

5 Alison's idea about looking after part-time workers is:
  a an idea she got from a different job.
  b an idea she got from her school.
  c her own idea.

6 The manager wants Alison to:
  a start work in May next year.
  b work as a manager next year.
  c work for two months next year.

Word Builder Multi-part verbs (2)

3 Match the beginnings (1–7) with the correct endings (a–g).

1 Our boss has asked us all to come _c_
2 I'll get ___
3 Thank you for your help and I look ___
4 If you want to teach technology, you have to keep ___
5 I'll be back in a minute so take ___
6 Jack has promised to help ___
7 There are three people in my class who I don't get ___

a on with.
b out with organising the school disco.
c up with some ideas to make more money.
d care of my bag, please.
e in touch with you as soon as I know which train I'll be on.
f up with the latest technology developments.
g forward to working with you again.

4 Complete the sentences with the correct words.

1 Can you take __care__ __of__ of my phone while I play football?
2 I have to get _____ _____ _____ Mr Smith about my interview.
3 I need a rest. I just can't come _____ _____ any new ideas for my article for the school magazine.
4 I'll help _____ _____ the cooking but I won't be able to stay and clean up, I'm afraid.
5 I work in the music business and I have to keep _____ _____ all the new bands and CDs.
6 You and Mark seem to be getting _____ very well _____ each other.
7 It's great that you'll be here in July. I look _____ _____ _____ you then.

Sentence Builder Asking what to do

5 Use the prompts to complete the polite questions.

1 What skills do I need?
you know / what skills / I need
Do you know what skills I need?

2 What should I write on my application form?
you advise / what / write on my application form

_____

3 Do you know any good websites to look at for summer work?
you recommend / some websites / look at for summer work _____

_____

4 How do I write a CV?
you tell / how / write a CV _____

_____

LESSON

30

GRAMMAR
Conditionals

① * **Match the beginnings (1–6) with the correct endings (a–f).**

1 If students don't know what they want to do _c_

2 If I work as a waiter this summer ___

3 If you were good at making money ___

4 If I lost my job ___

5 What will you say ___

6 What would you say ___

a your business would do better.

b if they asked you to work at night?

c we give them careers advice.

d I'd spend the rest of the summer on the beach.

e I'll be able to save £400.

f if they ask you how much money you want?

② * **Choose the correct answers to complete the sentences.**

1 If I work an extra two hours tonight, *I'll get*/I'd get £14 more than usual.

2 If I need a job next summer, I *don't work/ won't work* as a waitress.

3 If I *would be/was* a customer, I'd complain.

4 If I'm nice to people, they *will usually leave/ usually leave* a tip.

5 If I *wouldn't need/didn't need* the money, I *didn't do/wouldn't do* this job.

6 If I *don't write/won't write* down what people want, I usually make mistakes.

③ ** **Complete the sentences with the correct form of the verbs in brackets.**

1 The restaurant is always full on sunny days.

If it ___*is*___ (be) sunny, the restaurant is always full.

2 It's possible that you'll stay at home for the summer but I don't know what you will do.

What _____ (you / do) if you stay at home for the summer?

3 I've asked for a summer job but I'm not sure I want to work in the holidays.

If I don't get a summer job, I _____ (not be) too disappointed.

4 The school doesn't help students who miss the careers advice talks.

If students _____ (not go) to the careers advice talk, the school doesn't help them.

5 You don't meet anyone new because you don't go to any extra-curricular activities.

If you _____ (go) to some extra-curricular activities, you would meet some new people.

6 The reason you don't have time to write emails is because you play so many computer games.

If you _____ (not play) so many computer games, you would have more time to write emails.

7 I know you don't want to babysit on your own but what if I came with you?

_____ (you / babysit) for your aunt if I came with you?

④ *** **Complete the dialogue with a verb in the correct form.**

A: This French homework is really difficult.

B: What do you have to do?

A: Think of the next letter. L M M J …

B: Don't you know?

A: If I ¹ _*knew*_ , I wouldn't ask you.

B: Think. If you ² _____ about it, you will get the answer.

A: I am thinking. If I say 'please', ³ _____ me the answer?

B: No. If I tell you, you ⁴ _____ it.

A: I will, I will remember it. Of course I'll remember it. Please tell me. It's stupid homework. If I ⁵ _____ a teacher, I ⁶ _____ give my class homework like this. I'd give them something more useful.

B: This makes you think and it's fun. What have you been studying in French recently?

A: … Er, days of the week and months of the year.

B: Okay, I'll tell you the next letters but not the answer. L M M J V S D. And that's all there are. Seven. I'm going to make some tea. If you still ⁷ _____ the answer when I come back, I'll tell you.

A: Wait a minute, seven, seven days of the week, of course. Lundi, mardi, er, and the other days. Now, what about this? J F M A … What can that be?

Workshop 5

Writing

1 Order the parts (a–f) of the letter.

a _1_ Dear Sir / Madam,

b ___ I am in my final year at school and I will be doing my A levels this summer. I will then study history and French at Durham University. I speak French and some German and I am good at communicating and dealing with people.

c ___ Yours faithfully,
___ Martina Hindson.

d ___ I look forward to hearing from you.

e ___ I am writing ⁱ___to___ apply for the position of tour guide advertised in the Arun Weekly last weekend.

f ___ I am interested in working as a tour guide in ⁱⁱ_____ to practise my language skills and ⁱⁱⁱ_____ that I can share my love of the local area and its history with other people. I would also like to do the job ⁱᵛ_____ the experience it would give me, which would be good for my CV.

2 Complete the letter in exercise 1 with a word in each gap (i–iv).

3 Read the instructions and write a letter of application in your notebook. Write between 120 and 180 words.

Landscape Tours

Life guards wanted for outdoor swimming pool

Young people aged sixteen to thirty needed, seven days a week for July and August. You must have good skills and some experience.

Write now saying why you think you would be good for this job.

Speaking

1 Match the beginnings (1–7) with the endings (a–g).

1 Is it okay _e_
2 Can I ask you a ___
3 Do you ___
4 Can I ___
5 Do you think ___
6 Could you tell ___
7 Can you say ___

a look round?
b me when you could start?
c question?
d I could look round?
e if I sit down?
f what the most important skills you would need are?
g mind if I ask you a question?

2 **2.25** Use the prompts to make polite requests. Then listen to the conversation and check your answers.

1 could / tell / your / name / please
Could you tell me your name please?

2 is / okay / I / sit down
_____

3 think / I / take my jacket off
_____

4 mind / I / ask / you / few / questions
_____

5 could / tell / how / hear / about the job
_____

6 could / tell / what / part-time work / you do / before
_____

7 can / ask / how much money / got / at the Beach Café
_____

8 mind / I / not / answer that
_____

Check Your Progress 10

1 Careers **Complete the words with the correct letters.**

When I was young, I always loved drawing and clothes. I wanted a job in [1]a _ _ / d _ _ _ g _ and to be able to make my own clothes so I became a [2]f _ _ h _ _ _ d _ _ _ g _ _ _
My dad loves playing the guitar. He wanted to be a success in [3]s _ _ w b _ _ _ n _ _ _ but he didn't make it. He became a [4]j _ _ r _ _ _ _ s _ for a newspaper and now he interviews famous people. He's very glad his dream didn't come true.
My uncle was a [5]p _ _ _ c _ o _ _ _ c _ _ and, when he left his job, he became a [6]d _ _ _ c _ _ v _ like Sherlock Holmes.

/6

2 Reported questions **Complete the reported form of the questions and the polite requests.**

1 What time do you finish work?
My friend asked me _____ work.

2 Do you want to go out with me?
I asked a girl in my class _____ with me.

3 How much money have you got?
I asked my brother _____ got.

4 What questions did the interviewer ask you?.
My mum asked me _____.

5 Are you working hard?
My mum wanted to know _____ hard.

/5

3 Multi-part verbs (2) **Complete the sentences with the correct words.**

1 Where does Pete come _____ with all these great ideas?

2 I need three people to help me _____ in the office on Sunday.

3 Thank you for coming. I look forward to _____ you again soon.

4 I don't know how your grandfather keeps _____ with all the latest technical developments.

5 I can't be a babysitter. I don't know how to _____ care of children.

6 One of my best skills is that I can get _____ well with everyone.

7 Did Mrs Jenkins _____ in touch about the job I had the interview for?

/7

4 Conditionals **Use the prompts to make sentences.**

1 I / get / a present / pass my exams next month?
_____

2 you / have / lots of money / what car / you buy?
_____

3 I be / rich / I buy / a Mercedes
_____

4 where / you / go / you / want to go shopping
_____

/4

5 Purpose linkers **Complete the sentences with the correct purpose linkers.**

1 I would like to work for you _____ that I can practise speaking Spanish and French.

2 I am writing _____ apply for the waitress job advertised in the newspaper.

3 I am interested in working for you in _____ to get some experience working in an office.

4 He would like the job _____ some work experience.

/4

6 Polite requests **Choose the correct word to complete the sentences.**

1 Could you *tell/say* me why you are interested in journalism?

2 Is it *good/okay* if I answer my mobile?

3 Do you *mind/say* if I ask some questions?

4 Can you *say/tell* why you want this job?

/4

TOTAL SCORE **/30**

Module Diary

1 **Look at the objectives on page 77 in the Students' Book. Choose three and evaluate your learning.**

1 Now I can _____
well / quite well / with problems.

2 Now I can _____
well / quite well / with problems.

3 Now I can _____
well / quite well / with problems

2 **Look at your results. What language areas in this module do you need to study more**

Exam Choice 5

Reading

1 Read the text quickly and match the jobs (a–f) with the correct paragraphs (1–5). There is one extra job.

   a shop assistant   **d** cleaner
   b tour guide   **e** life guard
   c babysitter   **f** waiter/waitress

2 Read the text again and match the people below (a–f) with the best job descriptions for them from exercise 1. There is one extra person.

   a I'm an outgoing, lively person who always works hard. I like sports and maths but I'm happy to do anything. I am friendly and get on well with people. I can only work at the weekends or in the evenings as I am at school. I'm eighteen years old and will be going to university next year. _2_

   b I am a twenty-two year old student looking for a summer job. I am studying languages (French and German) and would like a chance to practise them while at work if possible. I am talkative and sociable and get on well with people. I am also interested in historical buildings in the local area.

   ___

   c I'm a quiet but reliable person. I work hard on my own and as part of a team. I would like a job at the weekend but I would prefer not to do anything too tiring as I do a lot of sports during the day. I come from a large family and am the oldest of four children and I enjoy being with young children. ___

   d I am seventeen years old and have had several part-time jobs in shops and restaurants. My favourite subjects at school are maths and technology. I am able to work as part of a team or independently and I am looking for evening or weekend work. I like to dress smartly and take care of my appearance. ___

   e I am a sixteen year old girl. I enjoy writing and have written several activities for the school magazine. I am looking for a job in which I would have a chance to use my writing skills and I can work in the evenings or at weekends. ___

   f I am a fit and healthy twenty-two year old man and I am very mature and responsible. I love sports, especially football, basketball and swimming. I am looking for work during the summer holidays and would like to do something outdoors. I can work any day of the week. ___

1 ___ We need a responsible young person to work from 8 p.m. until 12 a.m. on Saturdays. We have two young children aged two and four. They will be in bed before you arrive but you will need to be here to look after them if they wake up or if something happens. We have a collection of DVDs that you are welcome to watch, and we will take you home at the end of the evening by car. This is for one person only and you mustn't invite anyone else to join you. We prefer people who have younger brothers or sisters or who have experience of taking care of children.

2 ___ We need energetic, friendly young people to work at weekends. You must be hard working, polite and helpful at all times, even at the end of a busy day. No experience is needed but you will need to come to an interview and explain why you think you would be good at this job. Because alcohol is served in the restaurant, we can only employ people aged eighteen or over.

3 ___ We are looking for people aged eighteen to thirty to work for us for the summer. No experience is necessary but you must be a strong swimmer and already have, or be willing to take, the necessary life saving qualifications. You must also be totally reliable and we will be asking people you have worked for or your teachers from school to tell us about your character and abilities. We need people to work five days a week, including weekends. You will have two days off between Monday and Friday.

4 ___ We need people to work on Friday evenings and Saturdays. You should be good at dealing with people and able to work independently. You should also be good at doing simple calculations and it will be good if you have worked with money before. No experience is necessary as you will have one day of training in the shop before you start working alone. You should look smart and must be at least sixteen years old. You must be able to work hard as our supermarket gets very busy at these times.

5 ___ We need three people to work this summer. Good communication skills are essential and you should be friendly, smart and good at dealing with people. Speakers of other languages are especially important as we often have parties of French, German, Italian and Japanese visitors to show around the castle. However, we also need English speakers for our normal tours. You should already have a good knowledge of the castle's history and show a real interest in talking about it.

Listening

3 **2.26** Listen to an interview about helping school students to find work and put the topics they discuss in the order they talk about them.

a how they get the message to the students ___
b talking about yourself ___
c future plans ___
d how to find jobs ___
e a good CV ___
f looking right. ___
g differences between working and school ___

4 **2.26** Listen again and choose the correct answers.

1 At the moment, Roger is:
   a at school. b at university. c working.

2 To help students find work, the group:
   a puts articles in local newspapers.
   b goes round the country talking to individual students who need help.
   c gives ideas of good places for students to look.

3 Roger thinks that students who look into an interviewer's eyes when they are talking:
   a are more honest.
   b are more nervous.
   c are more likely to get the job.

4 Roger thinks that:
   a computing and films are not good interests to have.
   b doing extra-curricular activities may help people get jobs.
   c the film club and computer club are the most interesting extra-curricular activities to do.

5 The main differences between school and work are that:
   a you aren't told what to do as often at work.
   b you work harder at work.
   c you meet more people at work.

6 One thing the group want to do but haven't done yet is to:
   a write a magazine.
   b put videos of interviews on the internet.
   c start their own website.

Speaking

5 Order the words to make polite questions.

1 okay / drink / is / water / if / of / it / have / I / a / ?

_____

2 tell / how long / studying English / could / me / have been / you / you / ?

_____

3 you / outside school / say / how / you use / can / English / ?

_____

4 I / mind / this question / do / answer / you / if / ?

_____

5 please / something / do / I / could / think / you / say / ?

_____

6 **2.27** Look at exercise 5 and decide who says each question, an examiner (E) or a student (S). Then listen and check your answers to exercises 5 and 6.

1 _   2 _   3 _   4 _   5 _

Exam Choice 5

Use of English

7 Complete the second sentences so that they have the same meaning as the one above. Use between two and five words including the word in capitals.

1 I'm not very good at maths so I can't get a job in finance.
(WAS)
If _____ maths, I could get a job in finance.

2 In what way is construction different to engineering?
(BETWEEN)
What's the _____ construction and engineering?

3 Please contact me if you have any questions.
(TOUCH)
Please _____ me if you have any questions.

4 'I took eight exams at the end of the school year,' said Jake.
(HAD)
Jake said that _____ eight exams at the end of the school year.

5 Why would you like to work in farming?
(WHY)
Could you tell _____ to work in farming?

6 How should I start this application letter?
(TO)
Could you advise _____ this application letter?

7 My boss thinks of some amazing ways to make money.
(COMES)
My boss _____ some amazing ways to make money.

8 Which subjects do you want to drop? asked Ben.
(WANTED)
Ben asked me which _____ to drop.

9 Do you think you could look after two young children?
(CARE)
Do you think you could _____ two young children?

10 'Does your brother belong to the army cadets?' asked Elsa.
(MY)
Elsa asked me _____ to the army cadets.

Writing

8 Match the beginnings to the endings.

1 There are lots of great activities at our school such as ___

2 Some people go to something different every day, like ___

3 Not everything takes place at school, for example ___

a Jack, who goes to history club, poetry club, chess, dancing and the school choir.

b last week, we went to a museum to learn about local history.

c climbing, kayaking and sailing.

9 Write a blog post about extra-curricular activities at your school. Use one of the titles below for your blog.

1 A great choice
2 Really interesting
3 We learn so much

Write between 100 and 150 words.

TOPIC TALK – VOCABULARY

1 Complete the words.

¹c	i	n	e	m	a	
²d	n					
³m	s					
⁴s	p					
⁵m	i					
⁶o	r					
⁷a	a					
⁸b	t					
⁹a	i					
¹⁰c	o					
¹¹p	n					

1 A place which people go to watch films.
2 A contemporary _____ performance.
3 A place to visit where you can see old, interesting objects
4 A kind of art where the artist makes shapes from wood, metal or other materials.
5 Films or plays with songs in them.
6 A musical play in which all the words are sung.
7 You can see 4 and 11 here. (3-7)
8 A performance in which the story is told by music and dancing with no words.
9 An exciting kind of film.
10 A funny story which makes you laugh.
11 Creating pictures using a brush and colours.

2 Choose the correct words to complete the sentences.

1 I've been asked to be in the school play but I can't create/*act*/draw.
2 The music teacher wanted us to compose/paint/act a piece of music for the school orchestra.
3 I don't know how people can create/draw/paint such great sculptures from ice.
4 I'm trying to write/compose/draw a picture of my house.
5 Does anyone want to act/create/play in the school orchestra?
6 You should compose/take/sing in the school choir.
7 This is a great exhibition. Some of the Year twelve students make/take/draw great photos.
8 I've got some good tunes for the band but I need someone to draw/write/take some lyrics.

3 Complete the adjectives with the correct letters.

A: That film was great.
B: Yes, it was ¹a _m a z i n g_. Really ²e _ t _ _ t _ _ n _ _ _.

A: I liked the concert.
B: So did I. It was ³b _ _ l _ _ a _ _.

A: That was a great comedy.
B: Yes. It was really ⁴f _ _ n _ and ⁵o _ _ g _ n _ _.

A: The photographs were interesting.
B: Yes but the ones of wars and disasters were quite ⁶d _ _ t _ _ b _ _ _.

A: They were ⁷s _ _ c _ _ n _ but also very ⁸m _ v _ _ _.

A: Did you like the sculptures?
B: Not really. They were a bit ⁸w _ _ r _.

A: That concert was ⁹a _ f _ _.
B: Why did you go? Classical music is always ¹⁰d _ l _.

A: No, it isn't. Sometimes it can be really ¹¹i _ _ p _ r _ _ _.

4 Complete the sentences with the words below. There are two answers you can choose from for each gap. Try to make the sentences true for you.

awful best brilliant cinema compose music concert draw film going to concerts ~~is~~ ~~isn't~~ going to plays theatre worst

There ¹ _is / isn't_ a lot on where I live.
I go to the ² _____ quite often.

I prefer seeing films to ³ _____.
I'd love to be able to ⁴ _____.

The ⁵ _____ thing I've been to recently was a ⁶ _____. It was really ⁷ _____.

31

SKILLS

Reading

1 Read review one about a musical called *Thriller* and choose the correct answers.

1 It's about *Madonna/Michael Jackson.*

2 It started in *2009/2010.*

3 The show *was a good length/too long.*

4 *One person plays/Several people play* the lead part in the play.

5 The show is about the person's *life/music.*

6 The people watching the show were *happy/disappointed.*

7 The review is generally *positive/negative.*

REVIEW ONE

If someone wanted to make a musical about a famous person, then Michael Jackson would be an obvious person to choose so it's not surprising that one of the most successful London musicals of recent years has been *Thriller*. The show opened in January 2009 and the plan was for it to continue until the summer of that year. However, after Michael's death in June 2009, interest in the show grew and you can still see it today.

A number of different actors play the lead role in the show. All of them are excellent in different ways. Interestingly, the show hasn't tried to find actors who look or sound like Michael and that's probably a good idea. One of the best actors in the show is Denise Pearson who used to be a member of the pop group Five Star. She sings *The Way You Make Me Feel* and she sings it brilliantly. In fact, all the songs are sung well and the makers of the show have chosen a good selection of Michael's greatest hits from all stages of his life. The dancing is even better, with superb choreography, and the special effects are amazing with wonderful sets and lighting. They all help to make the evening truly magical.

I was a little disappointed that there was no real story of his life. I feel we needed to know, not everything, but a little about how he was feeling and what he was doing when he sang each song. The show was a perfect length at just over two hours. In fact, I didn't want it to stop and I don't think another twenty minutes would be too much.

Apart from that, it was a great night out. The audience left the theatre with smiles on their faces, knowing that the money they had paid for their tickets was very well spent.

REVIEW TWO

There are some things about *Thriller*, the musical, that you can't complain about. It is a great show with brilliant choreography, excellent dancers and amazing sets and special effects. However, it wasn't all good.

Firstly, the people chosen to play Michael were a strange collection. Why did they choose people completely different from him, including one woman and someone who couldn't sing? A better idea would be to play Michael Jackson's songs and just have people dancing to them.

I was also disappointed with the choice of songs. In my opinion, there were too many early hits. As the show was half an hour too long, I think they should cut out five of them.

Despite not enjoying the singing, I was pleased to see that the show concentrated on the songs and not Michael's life. His songs are what his fans want to remember him for and that's what the show gives them.

Overall, then, not bad but it could be better and I'm glad I got a free ticket. The price other people had to pay to see this show was shocking.

2 Read both reviews carefully. For each review, are the things below listed as arguments for (F) or against (A) the musical?

	Review one	Review two
1 choice of actors	_F_	___
2 choice of songs	___	___
3 choreography	___	___
4 dancing	___	___
5 length of the show	___	___
6 sets and special effects	___	___
7 singing	___	___
8 the fact that there was no plot	___	___
9 ticket prices	___	___

Word Builder Noun + noun

3 Complete the sentences with the words below.

actor   band   critic   ~~hits~~   industry   music   musical   screen   song

1 I'm going to buy Rhianna's greatest __hits__ album.
2 I'd love to go to a West End _____ but the tickets are really expensive.
3 One theatre _____ was quite negative about the play but most reviews were very good.
4 The music _____ has to do something about illegal downloads of songs.
5 I heard a great pop _____ on the radio but I don't know who sang it.
6 I wouldn't want to be in a boy _____ even if it made me rich. I prefer 'real' groups like Metallica.
7 The lead _____ in the film was good but the plot was awful.
8 Most films look much better in the cinema than on a TV _____.
9 I prefer rock _____ to pop or jazz.

Sentence Builder Contrast linkers

4 Complete the sentences with *although, despite* and *however*. One word can be used twice.

1 I enjoyed the show. _However_, the tickets were too expensive.
2 _____ I enjoyed the show, I felt that the tickets were too expensive.
3 _____ enjoying the show, I felt that the tickets were too expensive.
4 I enjoyed the show, _____, I felt that the tickets were too expensive.
5 I enjoyed the show _____ it being very expensive.

5 Complete the sentences so that they mean the same as the one below.

The actors were good dancers but none of them were good at singing.

1 Although ____the actors were good dancers____, ____none of them were good at singing____.
2 _____. However, _____.
3 _____, although _____.
4 Despite _____, _____.

Writing

6 Write the name of a film you know and answer the questions.

Film: _____
Which word best describes:
1 the plot: *awful/weird/brilliant/inspiring*
2 the lead actors: *boring/not bad/amazing/funny*
3 the special effects: *none/dull/okay/spectacular*
4 the script: *poor/funny/interesting/original*
5 the length: *too short/just right/too long*

7 Use your ideas from exercise 6 to write a short review (a paragraph) of the film in your notebook.

32

GRAMMAR
Past Conditional

Complete exercises A-B before you start this lesson.

A Rewrite the sentences using the word in brackets.

1 I took my umbrella because it was raining. (SO)

   It was raining so I took my umbrella.

2 The film was awful so we left the cinema before it finished. (BECAUSE)

   We _____

   _____

3 I didn't go to the play because I didn't have much money. (SO)

   I _____

   _____

4 I read the song lyrics because I wanted to understand what it was all about. (SO)

   I _____

   _____

5 The jokes weren't funny so I didn't laugh. (BECAUSE)

   I _____

   _____

6 I didn't want the whole album so I downloaded three songs from it. (BECAUSE)

   I _____

   _____

7 The musical was good because the cast were brilliant singers. (SO)

   The _____

   _____

B Complete the sentences with *so that*, *although* or *when*.

1 __When__ I finished work, I went for something to eat.

2 I wrote down everything _____ I wouldn't forget.

3 I enjoyed the exhibition _____ I don't usually like modern art.

4 We bought tickets for the show early _____ we could get seats near the front.

5 _____ the special effects were good, the film was quite disappointing.

6 I was amazed _____ the lead singer left the band.

1 * Read the story and put the events (a-g) in the order they happened. There are two things that didn't happen.

If I hadn't gone to Nicola's party, I wouldn't have met Greg. If I hadn't met Greg, he wouldn't have told me about the summer job. If I hadn't got the summer job, I would have gone camping with Luke and Nick. If I'd gone camping with Nick and Luke, I'd have spent all my money. If I had spent all my money, I wouldn't have been able to buy a new laptop. If I hadn't bought a new laptop, all my photos would be on my old PC which crashed last night.

a I met Greg. ___

b I went camping with Nick and Luke. ___

c My PC crashed. ___

d I spent all my money. ___

e I went to Nicola's party. _1_

f I heard about the summer job. ___

g I bought a laptop. ___

2 ** Choose the correct answers.

1 If _b_ more time in Paris, I would have gone to the Museum of Modern Art.

   a I would have had

   b I had had

   c I have had

2 If I'd gone there, ___ the Van Gogh exhibition.

   a I'd see

   b I'd seen

   c I'd have seen

3 I might have gone to the National Gallery if I ___ lost in London.

   a had got

   b hadn't got

   c wouldn't have got

4 I'd have seen some great paintings if ___ able to find it.

   a I'd been

   b I was

   c I've been

5 I ___ to the Louvre if the queues had been shorter.

   a had gone

   b 'd have gone

   c 've gone

6 If I'd stayed in the queue, it ___ about three hours to get inside.

   a would have taken

   b had taken

   c would take

3 *** **Complete the second sentences so that they mean the same as the first.**

1 I didn't go to the party because I felt ill.
If *I hadn't felt ill*, I'd have gone to the party.

2 I never listened in art classes so I didn't learn much.
If _____ in art classes, I might have learned something.

3 I couldn't go to the art exhibition because it was only on from Monday to Friday.
I _____ to the art exhibition if it had been on at the weekend.

4 I had to walk home from the cinema because the play finished after the last bus had gone.
If the film had finished earlier, _____ to walk home.

5 I was bored last night because I didn't have anything to do.
If _____ something to do, I wouldn't have been bored last night.

6 I only went to the cinema because my friends wanted to see the film.
I wouldn't have gone to the cinema if my friends _____ to see the film.

4 *** **Complete the dialogues using the Past Conditional.**

1 A: I went to Jason's barbecue. It was great but I was cold in my T-shirt in the evening.
B: take a jumper / not be cold
If you'd taken a jumper, you wouldn't have been cold.

2 A: My grandfather had a painting by Picasso but he gave it away. He was very poor when he died.
B: not give it away / might not be poor when he died
_____

3 A: I went to a concert last week. I arrived late and had to stand right at the back. I couldn't see anything.
B: not be late / might have a better time
_____

4 A: I took lots of photos on holiday but they aren't very good. I think I need a better camera.
B: The weather was really bad, that's why they are so dark. have a better camera / not take better photos
_____

5 A: The exhibition was awful. I hated it.
B: That's because there was no one there to explain the paintings. there be an expert there / might understand them better
_____

Grammar Alive Regrets

5 **Look at the regrets and say what would have been different if he had or hadn't done these things.**

1 I didn't phone my mum when I was late.
She was angry with me.
If _____*I had phoned my mum when I was late,*_____
_____*she wouldn't have been angry with me.*_____

2 I ate too much last night.
I felt sick.
If _____

3 I cut my own hair.
My friends laughed at me.
If _____

4 I didn't study hard.
I failed my exams.
If _____

5 I didn't remember my girlfriend's birthday.
She left me.
If _____

6 I broke a window with my football.
I had to spend all my money on a new one.
If _____

1 Put the words below in the correct category.

> composer   dance   director   ~~drawing~~   music   musician   opera
> painting   photography   playwright   sculpture   theatre

Visual arts	Performing arts	Artists
drawing _____	_____ _____	_____ _____
_____ _____	_____ _____	_____ _____

Talk Builder Opinions: Reasons and examples

2 2.28 Complete the opinions with the words and phrases below. Then listen to check your answers.

> another example is   another reason   because
> because of   for example   like   main reason
> ~~my opinion~~   take   the reason for that

A: Why do you like Van Gogh?

B: In [1] _my opinion_ he's the best artist who ever lived [2] _____ his use of colour and his amazing way of seeing things. His best paintings, [3] _____ Sunflowers and his Café Terrace At Night, are very realistic but also very different to a photo. [4] _____ is that he could see things that other people couldn't see.

A: What's so good about Hollywood action films?

B: The [5] _____ I like them is that they are great fun. You can forget all about your worries for two hours. [6] _____ why I like them is that you never know what is going to happen next. [7] _____ Speed, [8] _____.You know Keanu Reeves and Sandra Bullock will live but it's a shock when his friend dies. [9] _____ the Indiana Jones films. They're quite old but they're brilliant [10] _____ the action never stops.

3 2.29 Listen to two people discussing sculptures and complete the table with the information below. You have to use the sculptures twice in the table.

> All the different reflections   Statue of Cary Grant   ~~'Follow me'~~
> It's natural   It's not very imaginative.
> It's weird and difficult to understand.   The details
> You see other people/everyone interacts

Katie		Jamie
'Follow me'	sculpture he/she likes	_____
_____	main reason for liking it	_____
_____	other reasons for liking it	_____
_____	sculpture he/she doesn't like	_____
_____	reasons for not liking it	_____

4 2.29 Complete the sentences from the conversation with the correct words. You can see the first letter of each word. Then listen again to check your answers.

1 I _n_ m_____ o_____, it's really interesting because of all the different reflections you can see.

2 A_____ r_____ I l_____ i_____ i_____ t_____ you can see the reflections of other people.

3 T_____ m_____ r_____ I l_____ the statue is that it looks so natural.

4 A_____ e_____ is the book he's carrying.

5 Personally, I didn't like the mirror labyrinth much. T_____ r_____ f_____ t_____ is that I'm not really into modern art.

6 A lot of modern art l_____ 'Follow Me' is a bit weird and difficult to understand - i_____ m_____ o_____ anyway.

7 I didn't like it very much b_____ it's not very imaginative.

Check Your Progress 11

1 The arts **Complete the sentences with the correct words.**

1 I'm going to act in a real p_____ at the theatre.
2 My dream is to c_____ a great piece of music.
3 Wouldn't it be great to c_____ a sculpture out of a piece of wood?
4 I love sitting outside, d_____ what I see on a piece of paper.
5 With my new camera, I can t_____ wonderful photos.
6 I don't want to sing in the c_____. I want to play the violin in the o_____.

/6

2 The arts **Match the adjectives below with the sentences with the same meaning. There are two extra words.**

brilliant   disturbing   dull   funny   moving   shocking   weird

1 I didn't enjoy the musical because it was boring. _____
2 These paintings are really strange. _____
3 The film made me laugh a lot. _____
4 This CD is great. _____
5 It was a very sad story that really made me cry. _____

/5

3 Noun + noun **Choose the correct word to complete the sentences.**

1 The most important actor in a film is the *lead/head/top* actor.
2 A kind of music that lots of people like and is often heard on the radio is *top/pop/hop* music.
3 A group made up of all young, good-looking males who quite often don't play the music on their songs is called a *boy band/rock group/lead group*.
4 A musical at one of the theatres in the centre of London is a *Centre Town/West End/North Side* musical.
5 When you watch TV, you look at the *monitor/screen/speaker*. These are now much bigger than they were a few years ago.
6 A CD made up of the most successful songs by a singer or group is a greatest *tops/hits/pops* album.

/6

4 Contrast linkers **Complete the sentences with** *however*, *although* **or** *despite*.

1 The dancing is fantastic _____ the singing could be better.
2 _____ getting great reviews, not many people have been to see the new play.
3 The boy band look fantastic. _____ their singing could be better.
4 I didn't like the musical, _____ the good reviews.

/4

5 Past conditional **Complete the sentences with the correct form of the verbs in brackets.**

1 I _____ (go) to the party last week if I _____ (know) about it sooner.
2 If Leonardo da Vinci _____ (not paint) the Mona Lisa, he might _____ (not become) so famous.
3 I could _____ (sing) the song better if I _____ (not have) a cold on the night of the concert.

/6

6 Opinions: Reasons and examples **One word is missing in each sentence. Find out where it should be and write it.**

1 In ‸ opinion, modern art is rubbish. ___*my*___
2 I like this photo because the way the sunlight shines on the woman's face. _____
3 The main reason I like rock music that it's so exciting. _____
4 I prefer classical music to rock music it's more relaxing. _____

/3

TOTAL SCORE   **/30**

Module Diary

1 **Look at the objectives on page 85 in the Students' Book. Choose three and evaluate your learning.**

1 Now I can _____
well / quite well / with problems.
2 Now I can _____
well / quite well / with problems.
3 Now I can _____
well / quite well / with problems.

2 **Look at your results. What language areas in this module do you need to study more?**

Sound Choice 6

Sound Check

Say the words and expressions below.

a If I'd known it was so bad, I wouldn't have gone. If I'd had enough money I would have bought the watch (Exercise 1)

b My teacher asked me if I'd like to be in the school play. Dan asked Louisa where she had been. (Exercise 2)

c designing, sing, painting (Exercise 3)

d there, career, appear (Exercise 4)

e In my opinion, Hollywood films are boring. Could you tell me where the theatre is? (Exercise 5)

f calculation, technician, action (Exercise 6)

g science, script, choir (Exercise 7)

2.30 **Listen and check your answers. Which sounds and expressions did you have problems with? Choose three exercises to do below.**

1 **2.31** **Grammar - contractions Listen and repeat the complete sentences.**

1 If I'd known it was so bad, I wouldn't have gone.
2 If I'd had enough money, I would have bought the watch.
3 My brother would have come out tonight if he hadn't had so much work.
4 I'd have preferred it if we'd stayed at home.

2 **2.32** **Grammar - direct, indirect and reported questions intonation Listen and repeat the questions and reported forms.**

1 Would you like to be in the school play?
Could you tell me if you'd like to be in the school play?
My teacher asked me if I'd like to be in the school play.
2 Where have you been?
Could you tell me where you have been?
Dan asked Louisa where she had been.
3 Did your mum like the exhibition?
Do you know if your mum liked the exhibition?
I asked my friend if his mum had liked the exhibition.

3 **2.33** **Consonants - /ɪŋ/ Listen to nine words and write them down. Then listen again and repeat them.**

1 _designing_	5 _____
2 _____	6 _____
3 _____	7 _____
4 _____	8 _____

4 **2.34** **Vowels - /eə/, /ɪə/, and /ʊə/ Listen to the words and write them in the column with the same vowel sound.**

rep**air** /eə/	w**ei**rd /ɪə/	t**our** /ʊə/
there		

5 **2.35** **Expressions - sentence stress Listen to the expressions and <u>underline</u> the word(s) with the main stress. Then listen again and repeat.**

1 In <u>my</u> opinion, Hollywood films are <u>boring</u>.
2 Could you tell me where the theatre is?
3 I'd like to know how much I will earn.
4 The main reason I like this painting is the colour.
5 The reason for that is that I don't like action movies.
6 Do you know if you've got the job yet?

6 **2.36** **Difficult words - -tion and -cian Listen to the words and repeat them. Then write them in the correct column.**

- **tion**	**-cian**
calculation	_____
_____	_____
_____	_____
_____	

7 **2.37** **Difficult words - /s/, /sk/, /k/ and /tʃ/ Look at the words and decide how the *sc* or *ch* is pronounced. Then listen to check.**

<u>sc</u>ience, <u>sc</u>ript, or<u>ch</u>estra, <u>Ch</u>inese, <u>ch</u>oir, <u>ch</u>oreography, bea<u>ch</u>, <u>ch</u>ange, <u>sc</u>reen, <u>sc</u>ulpture, <u>sc</u>ene

/s/ _science,_ _____
/sk/ _____
/k/ _____
/tʃ/ _____

TOPIC TALK – VOCABULARY

1 **Match the subjects (1-8) with the descriptions (a-h).**

1 In this we dig up old things. _c_
2 We study the brain and how people are thinking. ___
3 We learn how to design buildings. ___
4 We learn how to help the planet and environment. ___
5 We look at plants. ___
6 We study climate and the weather. ___
7 We study space. ___
8 We study people in different societies. ___

a ecology
b anthropology
c archaeology
d botany
e astronomy
f psychology
g meteorology
h architecture

2 **Complete the words with the correct letters.**

A: I'm working with robots to see if we can create ¹a _r_ _t_ _i_ f _i_ c _i_ _a_ _l_
i _ _ _ l _ _ g _ n _ _

B: Really? I work with robots too but tiny little robots. We're trying to use ²n _ _ _ t _ _ h _ _ l _ _ _ in medicine.

A: So, we both work in ³r _ _ _ t _ _ _ but in different areas.

A: I'd like to work in the area of ⁴g _ _ _ t _ _ e _ g _ _ _ _ r _ _ _. I'm interested in finding ways to make it possible to grow plants in the desert.

B: Me too but I'd like to work in ⁵b _ _ - t _ _ h _ _ l _ _ _. It's very similar.

A: It must be great to be involved in ⁶s _ _ c _ t _ _ v _ _. I'd love to travel to the other planets but I'm sure I never will.

B: No, but you may be able to find out what it's like. In a few years, we'll have ⁷v _ _ t _ _ _ r _ _ l _ _ _ and you'll be able to go anywhere and see anything you want.

3 **Label the inventions.**

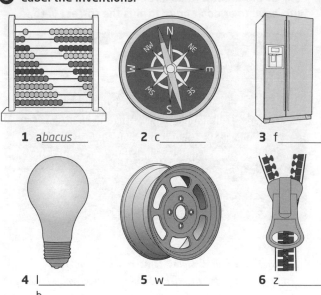

1 a_bacus_
2 c_____
3 f_____
4 l_____
   b_____
5 w_____
6 z_____

4 **Write full answers using the words given.**

1 A: What sciences have you studied?
   B: I / study / biology / chemistry
   I've studied biology and physics.

2 A: What do you think of science?
   B: (not) like / because / teachers / experiments
   _____

3 A: What would you like to learn more about?
   B: like / learn / ecology / astronomy
   _____

4 A: What do you think are the most important two inventions ever?
   B: think / two most important / wheel / microchip
   _____

5 A: Which two inventions make life more comfortable in your opinion?
   B: Two inventions / comfortable / fridge / car
   _____

6 A: What do you predict will become more important in the 21st century?
   B: predict / nanotechnology / genetic engineering
   _____

34

GRAMMAR
Past modals

REMEMBER

Complete exercises A–B before you start this lesson.

A Look at the theatre rules and complete the note with *have to* or *don't have to* plus the correct verb.

Theatre Rules

Please:

★ be in your seat five minutes before the show starts.

★ switch off all mobile phones when the lights go off (you can use them before and after the show).

★ be quiet during the show and don't leave your seats.

★ pay for your tickets (by credit card or in cash) at least twenty-four hours before the show starts or we may sell them to someone else.

Hi Mary

I'm writing about the play tomorrow evening. We ¹ *have to pay* for the tickets today or they might sell them. We ² _____ for them by credit card. I can go to the theatre and pay in cash if it's easier. We can meet at the theatre. I'll phone you when I arrive. We ³ _____ off our phones while the play is on but we ⁴ _____ them off until the lights go off. I'll tell you all my news after the play – we ⁵ _____ quiet while it's on! Oh, by the way. We ⁶ _____ in our seats five minutes before the play starts so don't be late! It starts at 8 p.m. and it only takes a few minutes to drive there so you ⁷ _____ home until 7.30 p.m.

B Use the words to make questions, sentences and short replies using the correct form of *should*.

I want to get fit. ¹What / I / do? *What should I do?*
²You / go / to a gym _____ .
³I / stop _____ smoking?
⁴Yes / you _____ . Smoking is very bad for you.
⁵And you / not / eat _____ fast food, either.
I've got exams next week. ⁶I / stay _____ awake all night studying?
⁷No / you _____ . ⁸You / get _____ a lot of sleep.
How much work ⁹I / do _____ every evening?
I think ¹⁰you / do _____ about three hours every evening but ¹¹you / have _____ a ten minute break every hour.

1 * **Match the beginnings (1–7) with the correct endings (a–g).**

1 Jackie and Tom were _b_
2 Our teacher told us we had ___
3 I was reading the book for ages but I wasn't ___
4 You should ___
5 Luckily, we didn't ___
6 Natalie couldn't ___
7 Everyone was amazed because my brother could ___

a have told us you were having problems at school.
b able to find work so why couldn't you?
c write his name when he was three.
d have to take a French test last year.
e to get more than sixty-five percent in our test.
f able to finish it because it was so long.
g remember any German when she went to Dresden.

2 * **Complete the sentences with the words below.**

could   couldn't   have   ~~had~~   should   was
were

1 At the school I went to, we ___*had*___ to study at least one science subject.
2 I was terrible at chemistry because I _____ understand it.
3 We _____ able to find our way home in the dark because we had a compass.
4 I was ill last week but I didn't _____ to go to the doctors. I just took an aspirin and went to bed.
5 I _____ have studied harder for my physics exam. I might have passed it.
6 When we walked into the house, we _____ smell gas so we quickly opened all the windows.
7 My uncle was really good at inventing things. He _____ able to make all sorts of things.

3 ** **Choose the correct answers.**

Do you remember *Jurassic Park*? In the film, scientists
[1] _a_ bring dinosaurs back to life using DNA. They
[2] ___ done it because they [3] ___ control the dinosaurs.
In the end, they [4] ___ leave the island where the
dinosaurs lived because it was too dangerous to stay
there. Well, now scientists in Japan are working on a
real life Jurassic Park. They have created mammoth
blood and now know how these hairy elephants [5] ___
to survive in very hot and cold temperatures. Soon,
they hope to have real live mammoths wandering
round. Perhaps they [6] ___ watched *Jurassic Park*
before they started on such a project.

1 **a** were able to **b** should have **c** had to

2 **a** had to **b** shouldn't have **c** could

3 **a** were able to **b** didn't have to **c** couldn't

4 **a** had to **b** should have **c** were able to

5 **a** could **b** had **c** were able

6 **a** were able to **b** should have **c** had to

4 *** **Complete the second sentence so that it has
the same meaning as the one above. Use two to
five words including the word in capitals.**

1 It wasn't a good idea for you to open up your
mobile phone and try to fix it.
(HAVE)
You _shouldn't have opened up_ your mobile
phone and tried to fix it.

2 It was possible for farmers to grow more food
using bio-technology.
(ABLE)
Farmers _____ more food
using bio-technology.

3 Our teacher told us to write a 200 word essay on
DNA for homework.
(HAD)
We _____ a 200 word essay
on DNA for homework.

4 I don't know why you didn't go to school by bicycle
today.
(SHOULD)
You _____ to school by
bicycle today.

5 It wasn't necessary for the police to use DNA
evidence as they knew who the criminal was.
(HAVE)
The police _____ DNA
evidence as they knew who the criminal was.

6 It wasn't possible for the scientists to control the
robots they had created.
(COULDN'T)
The scientists _____ the
robots they had invented.

Grammar Alive Obligations and mistakes

5 **Use the prompts to complete the questions.**

A: I worked in a shop last summer.

B: able / save / some money?
[1] _Were you able to save some money?_

A: A little but not much.

B: have / wear / uniform?
[2] _____

A: No but I had to wear a shirt and tie.

B: have / work / hard?
[3] _____

A: Yes, I did. I didn't rest at all.

B: able / go anywhere or / have / work all summer?
[4] _____

A: I didn't have a holiday at all because I agreed to
work the whole holiday.

6 **Now use the prompts to complete the answers.**

B: Are you glad you worked there?

A: No! should / look / for a better job.
[1] _I should have looked for a better job._

A: shouldn't / stay / there so long.
[2] _____

A: should / have / a holiday as well.
[3] _____

A: shouldn't / work / so hard.
[4] _____

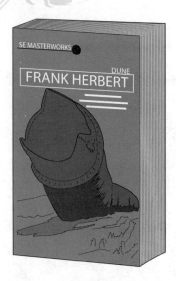

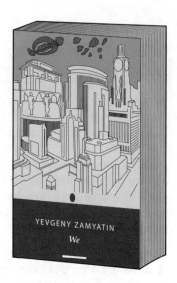

1 **2.38** Listen to a conversation about the history of science fiction and put the types of science fiction into the order they are talked about.

a Cyberpunk ___
b Dystopians ___
c Golden Age ___
d New Wave ___
e Postcyberpunk ___
f Proto science fiction _1_
g Pulp magazines ___
h Scientific Romance ___

2 **2.38** Listen again and make notes about the books, films and magazines.

1 *Utopia* by Thomas More:
   1516, about an imaginary, perfect world.

2 *The Lost World* by Sir Arthur Conan Doyle:
   _____

3 *Amazing Stories* by Hugo Gernsback:
   _____

4 *We* by Yevgeny Zamyatin:
   _____

5 *The Day of the Triffids* by John Wyndham:
   _____

6 *Dune* by Frank Herbert:
   _____

7 *The Matrix*:
   _____

8 *The Diamond Age* by Neal Stephenson:
   _____

Word Builder Multi-part verbs (3)

3 Complete the sentences with the correct form of the multi-part verbs below. Put the object in brackets in the middle of the verb where possible.

carry out   give up   hand out   let down   ~~think up~~

1 Science fiction is a great word but who (it) _thought it up?_
2 Tell your robot cleaner what to do and it will (all the tasks) _____ for you.
3 Here are some brochures about our gadgets. Could you (them) _____ to everyone here?
4 I'm not going to (my dreams of going back in time and meeting William Shakespeare) _____
5 The poor ending (the film) _____

Sentence Builder whatever/whenever, etc.

4 Complete the sentences with *wherever*, *whatever*, *whenever*, *whoever* or *however*.

1 **A:** Where do you want to go this evening?
   B: I don't mind. I'll go __wherever__ you want.
2 **A:** When do you want your DVD back?
   B: _____ you like. I've got lots of others I can watch.
3 **A:** That film was awful.
   B: I know. _____ recommended it to Clyde is weird.
4 **A:** Nothing will stop these aliens.
   B: No. They keep coming _____ we do to them.
5 **A:** We'll never be able to travel to other planets _____ much money we spend.
   B: Never say never. Scientists will find a way.

LESSON
36
GRAMMAR
Verbs with *-ing* or infinitive

1 * Choose the correct sentence.

1 **a** Tom loves watching football.
   b Tom can't stand watching football.

2 **a** Cathy's mum made her wear a hat.
   b Cathy's mum let her wear a hat.

No!

3 **a** Eric agreed to help.
   b Eric refused to help.

I ate all the cakes.

4 **a** Samantha avoided eating the cakes.
   b Samantha admitted eating the cakes.

5 **a** Ed asked Neil to help him with his homework.
   b Ed told Neil to do his homework on his own.

2 ** Complete the text about Michael Crichton with the correct form of the verbs in brackets.

Michael Crichton, who died in 2008, always
¹*enjoyed writing* (enjoy / write) even when he was
very young. At the age of fourteen, he ²_____
(manage / get) a column published in *The New York
Times*. It's not surprising that he ³_____ (plan /
study) literature. He went to Harvard University
although he ⁴_____ (decide / change) course
while he was there and got a degree in biological
anthropology. After that, he went on to study at
Harvard School of Medicine and it was at this time
that he started to write.

Crichton ⁵_____ (admit / be) a workaholic and
often slept for four hours a day or less while he
was writing. His books are full of scientific detail
⁶_____ (help / readers / understand) exactly how
the things he is describing work, for example how
dinosaurs could come back to life from DNA in
Jurassic Park. His books often describe problems that
can happen when scientists ⁷_____ (fail / think)
carefully about what they are doing, something he
believed was true in real life. Crichton also ⁸_____
(want / become) a film director and worked on a
number of films. He also ⁹_____ (help / create) the
television series *ER*.

3 *** Complete the sentences using the verbs below.

~~agreed~~ failed let loves managed
refused suggested

1 Okay, I'll meet you outside the cinema.
   Angela *agreed to meet me outside the cinema.*
2 No I won't lend you £10.
   My brother _____
3 I'm passionate about reading.
   Sue _____
4 I've done it! I've passed my physics test!
   Barbara _____
5 You can stay out until 11 p.m. on Friday.
   My parents _____
6 Why don't we go to the Science Museum at the weekend.
   Lottie _____
7 I can't find anyone who wants to come to my science club.
   Mel _____

Workshop 6

Writing

1 Complete the sentences from an opinion essay with the words below.

> according   benefits   cons   drawbacks
> hand (x 2)   impact   one   opponents   other   ~~pros~~
> sum   supporters   up   well

There are still arguments about the ^{1} _pros_ and ^{2}_____ of space travel.

On the ^{3}_____ ^{4}_____, ^{5}_____ say that it has led to satellites and other technology we use every day.

Other ^{6}_____ include other discoveries scientists have made by accident.

As ^{7}_____ as that, we may need to use our knowledge of space travel in the future if we have to escape from the Earth.

On the ^{8}_____ ^{9}_____, the ^{10}_____ of space travel point out its ^{11}_____. ^{12}_____ to them, the money we spend on space travel could be used to find clean energy.

To ^{13}_____ ^{14}_____, space travel could be important even if we can't say what ^{15}_____ it will have on our lives yet.

2 Match the parts of an opinion essay (1-4) with the information (a-d) that you will write in it.

'Artificial Intelligence may lead to many unknown dangers.'

1 Introduction _c_

2 Reasons for ___

3 Reasons against ___

4 Conclusion ___

    a Say what supporters of Artificial Intelligence believe.

    b Give a very short summary of the arguments for and against and give your opinion and the reasons for it.

    c Explain what Artificial Intelligence is and explain that there are different opinions about it.

    d Say what opponents of Artificial Intelligence believe.

3 Write an opinion essay on Artificial Intelligence in your notebook. Write between 120 and 180 words.

Speaking

1 Match the beginnings (1-11) with the endings (a-k).

1 Hi, _e_

2 Today we're going ___

3 First of all, let's ___

4 What I ___

5 So, the next ___

6 Now, ___

7 To start ___

8 That brings ___

9 So, to sum ___

10 Thanks very much ___

11 Has anybody got ___

    a mean is …

    b for listening to us.

    c up …

    d any questions?

    e everybody.

    f with …

    g look at …

    h question is …

    i to talk about …

    j us to …

    k let's look at …

2 (2.39) Complete the sentences with the words below. Then listen to check your answers.

> ~~can see~~   Now let's   brings us   let's look
> start with   next question   mean   sum up

1 Hi, everybody. As you _can see_ from the picture, today we're going to talk about communication.

2 First of all, _____ at traditional forms of communication.

3 When I say 'snail mail', what I _____ is traditional, non-electronic mail. Letters, postcards and things like that.

4 So, the _____ is, what is the most popular form of communication amongst teenagers?

5 _____ look at the internet.

6 To _____, we're going to show you a short history of texting.

7 That _____ us to social networking websites and Twitter.

8 So, to _____, communication has changed completely in the last ten years and it will probably change completely again in the next ten.

Check Your Progress 12

1 Inventions Match the inventions with the descriptions.

abacus battery compass gun light bulb match
microchip penicillin

1 It helps us to find out which way to go. _____
2 It helps us to stop diseases. _____
3 You can use it to start a fire or light a candle. _____
4 You can do simple maths on this. _____
5 When you put electricity into it, you get light. _____
6 This gives electricity to machines and makes them work. _____
7 It's tiny and found in most modern electrical goods. _____
8 You can use it to kill people or animals. _____

/8

2 Science/Social Science Choose the correct word to complete the sentences.

1 We did an interesting experiment in *chemistry/ archaeology* today.
2 I would like to be a doctor, so am going to study *geology/medicine* at university.
3 *Archaeology/Architecture* is a science where you design buildings.
4 *Economics/Ecology* is the study of the way in which money and goods are produced and used.
5 *Botany/Geology* is the scientific study of plants.

/5

3 Past modals Complete the text.

able could had have should

Scientists were ¹_____ to get a man on the moon in 1969 but, perhaps they ²_____ have spent the money on something more useful. However, the scientists ³_____ to do what the politicians told them.
After a few more trips to the moon, the politicians ⁴_____ relax again, knowing that they had 'won' the 'space race'. Scientists started thinking about sending spaceships to Mars. This time, though, they didn't ⁵_____ to worry about sending people there ...

/5

4 Multi-part verbs (3) Complete the sentences with a particle in the correct place. Use *down*, *out* or *up*.

1 Look at all these amazing ideas. Who thought them?
2 When we got to the exhibition, two men were handing free gadgets to everyone..
3 You used to have great plans for creating new plants. What happened? Have you given them?
4 The scientists had some great ideas but they were let by the government who refused to give them enough money to finish their experiments.

/4

5 *whatever/whenever*, etc. Match the beginnings (1–4) with the correct endings (a–d).

1 I go ___   a whenever I feel like it.
2 I do ___   b whoever has a friendly face.
3 I get up ___   c whatever I want.
4 I speak to ___   d wherever I like.

/4

6 Verbs with *-ing* or infinitive Choose the correct answers.

1 Our teacher let ___ our homework at school.
  a start   b us start   c us to start
2 My dad offered ___ me with my science project.
  a to help   b helping   c help
3 Louisa admitted ___ her homework from the internet.
  a copy   b copying   c to copy
4 My brother asked me ___ him to a football match.
  a to take   b take   c taking

/4

TOTAL SCORE /30

Module Diary

1 Look at the objectives on page 93 in the Students' Book. Choose three and evaluate your learning.

1 Now I can _____
  well / quite well / with problems.
2 Now I can _____
  well / quite well / with problems.
3 Now I can _____
  well / quite well / with problems

2 Look at your results. What language areas in this module do you need to study more?

Exam Choice 6

Reading

1 Read the text on the right quickly and match the ideas to the correct films.

1 *Enchanted* ___
2 *Across the Universe* ___
3 *Tangled* ___
4 *Burlesque* ___
5 *Hairspray* ___

a A man plays the part of a woman.
b It has some real actors and some characters are drawn.
c Someone from one country moves to another.
d It cost a lot of money to make.
e It was one person's first ever film.

2 Read the text again and choose the correct answers.

1 What kind of text is this from?
   a a blog about films
   b an article about different kinds of films
   c a review of some films at the cinema at the moment
   d a news story about successful films

2 The writer's intention is to:
   a discuss why films are so successful.
   b describe what makes a successful film.
   c recommend films to watch.
   d criticise reviewers who he/she disagrees with.

3 The writer's view about *Enchanted* is that:
   a there's nothing bad about it at all.
   b Susan Sarandon should have had a bigger part.
   c the acting is better than the singing.
   d it's good but the plot is too childish.

4 *Across the Universe*:
   a is about The Beatles.
   b was made in the 1960s.
   c has a simple story line.
   d shows real, historical events.

5 When talking about *Tangled*, the writer says that he/she:
   a doesn't like any of the songs in the film.
   b disagrees completely with the reviewers.
   c likes one of the songs from the film.
   d liked the film although not the plot.

6 We know from what the writer says about *Burlesque*:
   a his/her opinion about the songs.
   b his/her opinion of Cher's singing abilities.
   c his/her opinion of the lead actors in the film
   d what happens to Christina Aguilera's character after she meets Cher.

7 *Hairspray* has been made into:
   a a film and a play.
   b two films and a play.
   c two plays and a film.
   d two films and two plays.

My favourite films

I love films so, today, I'm going to write about some of my favourites of the last few years, films which make perfect Friday evening viewing with family or friends. See what you think.

1 Enchanted

A great cast and a nice mix of live action, cartoons and computer effects. Don't worry that it's about princesses and talking animals. We all love being a child at times and this is a fairy story that everyone can enjoy. The lead actors are all perfect in their parts. Also worth looking out for is Susan Sarandon. Her part of an evil queen is small but perfectly played. The songs are also great and make you think back to the Disney classics such as *Snow White* and *Sleeping Beauty*.

2 Across the Universe

Reviews for this film were mixed but it's an interesting film with an excellent soundtrack. The plot is a little confusing. A lot of real events from the 1960s are shown and not explained very well. The story follows an artist from Liverpool as he goes to the USA to look for his father. It isn't just a history of the 1960s and it certainly isn't about the Beatles but it sometimes feels as if it was made in the 1960s – that's a good thing in my opinion!

3 Tangled

Okay, it's a cartoon but, amazingly, it is the second most expensive film ever made so there must be something special about it. Reviews have been very positive although some said that the songs are not memorable, which is probably true. However, I see the light is really lovely and I have sung that in the bath more than once! Even if you don't see *Tangled* for its songs, try to watch it for the special effects and the great plot.

4 Burlesque

Completely different to the other films here, this is the story of Ali, who moves to Los Angeles to find work in a nightclub. Ali is played by Christina Aguilera and the club owner by Cher. Cher is a wonderful actress who I always enjoy watching and Christina Aguilera is one of my favourite singers. Despite getting some poor reviews, the film won a Golden Globe as did one of the songs from the soundtrack. This is Christina Aguilera's first film and she is excellent. In fact, she and Cher are the reason I like this so much.

5 Hairspray

Hairspray was first made into a film in 1988 starring Ricki Lake. It was then turned into a musical play and that was also a success, so it was no surprise when a musical version of the film came out. The lead role is played by Nikki Blanksy and her mother is played by … John Travolta. The whole cast are excellent and the songs are superb. If you only watch one of the films here, make it this one. You won't be disappointed.

Listening

3 🔊 **2.40 Listen to an interview about art and match the artists to the paintings.**

a	Kandinsky	1	The Black Square ___
b	Leger	2	The Snail ___
c	Malevich	3	On White ___
d	Matisse	4	Onement 1 ___
e	Mondrian	5	Composition 10 ___
f	Newman	6	Counter-Composition V ___
g	Van Doesburg	7	Railway Crossing ___
h	Whistler	8	Black and Gold: The Falling Rocket ___

4 🔊 **2.40 Listen again and make notes of the interviewer's thoughts about each painting.**

1 The Black Square: *There's no artistic skill - he (the interviewer) could have painted it.*

2 The Snail: _____

3 On White: _____

4 Onement 1: _____

5 Composition 10: _____

6 Counter-Composition V: _____

7 Railway Crossing: _____

8 Black and Gold: The Falling Rocket: _____

Speaking

5 🔊 **2.41 Complete the text about a girl discussing music in an exam. Then listen to check.**

In my [1]o_____, older rock music is better than music made now.

[2]F_____ example, some of the songs that The Beatles sang nearly fifty years ago still sound great and fresh when you hear them on the radio.

The [3]m_____ reason I like rock music is [4]t_____ there are many different sounds all being played at the same time and you hear something different each time you listen.

[5]A_____ reason I like it is that it is good to listen to, good to dance to, good to sing or just to have in the background.

I love the classic groups [6]l_____ Pink Floyd, The Doors and Led Zeppelin.

The song I would choose is Stairway to Heaven. The [7]r_____ for that is that it is a mixture of different styles.

Exam Choice 6

Use of English

6 Read the text and choose the correct answers.

1. **a** battery   **c** compass
      b button   **d** bulb
2. **a** wherever   **c** whenever
      b whoever   **d** whatever
3. **a** artificial   **c** genetic
      b virtual   d invented
4. **a** set   **c** cast
      b plot   **d** made
5. **a** Although   **c** However
      b Despite   **d** Though
6. **a** thought up   **c** given up
      b handed out   **d** let down
7. **a** main   **c** special
      b lead   **d** hit
8. **a** could   **c** should
      b had   **d** able
9. **a** hasn't had   **c** doesn't have
      b hadn't had   **d** wouldn't have had
10. **a** to wait   **c** wait
       b us to wait   **d** us wait

INVASION from a different reality

Imagine a world that could be yours just by pressing a [1]_____ . A world you could escape to at any time. A world where you could do [2]_____ you wanted. A world you control. This kind of [3]_____ reality world is the subject of a new film by Ben Lemming. It is [4]_____ twenty years in the future and everyone has their own imaginary world to relax in after work. One man who does this is Jack, the hero of the film. [5]_____, Jack soon starts to realise that something strange is happening when he sees people from one world in another. How is this possible and what does it mean?

Ben has [6]_____ an amazing storyline and the acting and [7]_____ effects are also great. How was he [8]_____ to write such a wonderful screenplay? He says it is because of his background. He studied information technology at university and has worked on virtual worlds. If he [9]_____ that experience, he wouldn't have been confident that his stories were believable. I saw the film last night with other film reviewers – all except the last fifteen minutes. Ben is making [10]_____ until the film comes out in August before we can know how it finishes.

Writing

7 Choose the correct contrast linkers to complete the sentences.

Mamma Mia

Good things	Bad things
Great songs	Badly sung
Fun storyline	A bit too obvious
Good actors	Not always right for the parts
Beautiful photography	Poor choreography

1 I love Abba's songs *although/however/despite* they weren't well sung in this film.
2 *However/Although/Despite* being fun, the storyline was a bit too obvious.
3 The actors were good. *Despite/Although/However*, they weren't always right for the parts they were playing.
4 *Although/However/Despite* the photography was beautiful, the choreography wasn't very good.

8 Think of a film you have seen. Write a list of good and bad points similar to those above and then write a review using contrast linking words. Write between 120 and 180 words.

BIG EVENTS

Task: Find out about the 2008 Olympic Games in Beijing
Tools: www.olympic.org/olympic-games
Skills: Finding specific information on a website and using a search box versus a sitemap

Before you start

1 **What do you know about the Olympic Games? Answer the questions.**

1 When do the summer Olympics usually take place?

_____

2 In which month is the winter Olympics?

_____

3 Where were the 2008 and the 2012 summer Olympics?

_____

4 Which of the sports below are not Olympic sports today? Tick (✓) or cross (✗).

running ☐   sailing ☐   skiing ☐   boxing ☐
baseball ☐   table tennis ☐   water-skiing ☐

Research

2 **Go to www.olympic.org/olympic-games and find the answers to the questions in Exercise 1. Use methods A and B below. Which method is quicker and easier for you?**

A Use the *search box*. Search boxes are usually at the top right-hand side of a web page. Type these words to help you answer question 3 in Exercise 1.
2008 summer Olympics
2012 summer Olympics

B Use the *sitemap*. Many websites have a sitemap which can help you search. The sitemap can be in different places. Sometimes it is in the left-hand menu, sometimes in the top menu and sometimes in the bottom menu. On the official Olympic website home page, it is in the bottom menu.

Tip!

When you are looking for specific information, e.g. the name of an athlete, the search box can help you find it quickly. If you want more general information, e.g. information about the events at the summer Olympics, you can find it more quickly using the sitemap.

Task

3 **Imagine that you and a friend had tickets to attend one sporting event at the Beijing Olympics. Use the Olympics website and follow the steps below:**

* Find the page for the Beijing Olympic Games
* Find the list of sporting events at the Olympics – the heading is *All sports events*
* Select the sport that you saw and click on the heading
* Use the information on the site to complete the report below – you can find lists of results and see photos and videos on the site

Report on: [Name of event]

Countries/athletes involved:

Medalists:

Was it an exciting event? Why?

Do you think the winner deserved to win?

How did you feel while you watched the video?

4 **What did you think about the Olympic Games website? Was it easy to find information? Write two things that you liked about the website and two things to improve.**

_____

_____

_____

_____

Review

In this task I have:

* researched the 2008 Olympic Games
* written a report about an Olympic event.

111

HOUSES

Task: Find out about volunteering to help build houses
Tools: www.habitat.org/eurasia
Skills: Navigating a website to find specific information

Before you start

1 Answer the questions about voluntary work.

1 Have you ever worked as a volunteer?

2 How many voluntary organisations in your country can you think of?

Research

2 Go to **www.habitat.org/eurasia**. **Click on the heading 'Learn about Habitat' and then click on the heading 'Who we are' on the drop-down menu.**

3 Use the information in the 'Who we are' section to answer questions 1–4.

1 What does the organisation *Habitat for Humanity* do?

2 How many homes has *Habitat for Humanity* helped to build since 1976?

3 Who participates in building the homes?

4 In how many countries in Europe and Central Asia does Habitat for Humanity work?

Tip!

When you visit a website, you usually begin at the *Home page*, or *Home*. At the top of the Home page, there is usually a menu with tabs. One of the tabs on the menu often has information about the organisation, e.g. *About Us* or *Who we are*.

Task

4 You are now going to find out about some people who worked on a project for *Habitat for Humanity* in South Africa. Click on *Volunteer Stories* on the menu panel on the left, then click on *South Africa*. Answer the questions.

1 How long did it take to build the eight new homes at Orange Farm?

2 Who is Nacho Maquinay? How does he feel about his experience?

3 Which company does *Habitat for Humanity* have as a partner in South Africa? What does this company produce?

5 Would you like to work on a *Habitat for Humanity* project as a volunteer? Why/ Why not? (You can use information on the website to help you decide, or to explain your decisions.)

6 Share your answer with your teacher and the other students in your class.

Review

In this task I have:
- **researched a non-governmental organisation (NGO), and read testimonials**
- **written a paragraph using information from a website.**

HEROES

Task:	Find out about a famous movie character and write a character profile
Tools:	www.filmsite.org/100characters.html
	www.rottentomatoes.com/news/1863943/the_100_greatest_characters_of_the_decade
	www.simple.wikipedia.org
Skills:	Finding and using information online for a writing task

Before you start

1 Decide who is your favourite film character from an English-speaking film. To help you choose, look at the lists of characters on the websites below.

www.filmsite.org/100characters.html
www.rottentomatoes.com/news/1863943/
the_100_greatest_characters_of_the_decade

Research

2 Find out more information about your character. Go to the websites in Exercise 1 and search for your character. Then go to www.simple.wikipedia.org and search for your character. Use the information on this website to answer the questions.

1 What film is the character from?
_____

2 What is the character like, e.g. looks, personality?
_____

3 Why is this character a hero?
_____

4 Which actors have played this role?
_____

Task

3 Use your notes from Exercise 2 to write a profile of your character. Write a short paragraph explaining who he/she is and why you think this person is a hero.

Tip!

Simple English Wikipedia www.simple.wikipedia.org is a good website for English language learners. You can copy language from a site if you acknowledge the source (if you say where it comes from), like this:

Darth Vader is the most evil character in the *Star Wars* films. *'He wears a black uniform and a black cape. He also has a mask that lets him breathe, but the mask makes his breath noisy.'* The noise he makes is terrifying.

[from www.simple.wikipedia.org/wiki/
Darth_Vader 22 July 2011]

To acknowledge an online source:

- Put the copied text into quotation marks (')
  and/or *italics*
- Add the full url (web address) of the page you
  found the text
- Add the date you visited the website

4 Give your paragraph to the other students in your class to read. Which character do most of the class like best?

Review

In this task I have:
- **researched a famous film character**
- **written a short profile.**

HABITAT

Task: Look at the features on a company's Facebook page and write a short review of it
Tools: www.nordicvisitor.com www.facebook.com/nordicvisitor
Skills: Finding specific information on a web page, and exploring and evaluating a social networking site

Before you start

1 Go to www.nordicvisitor.com. Which places can you visit with this tour company? Where would you like to visit?

2 Explore the Facebook page for *Nordic Visitor* www.facebook.com/nordicvisitor

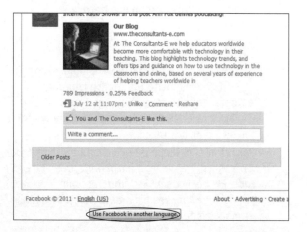

Tip!
You can change the language on Facebook to English by clicking on the link at the bottom of the page.

Research

The *Wall*

The *Wall* often includes comments and photos from the company and from their clients. It is usually the page you see first. To see if a wall is active, look at how often and when people last posted comments.

3 Look at the wall on the *Nordic Visitor* facebook page. Can you find these things?

1 travel information and updates
2 customers' messages
3 customers' photos
4 customers' opinions
5 company links and photos
6 advertisements of new products

Task

4 Look at the features (1-6) on Facebook and match them with the things they do (a-f).

1 the 'like' feature ___   4 info ___
2 photos ___   5 reviews ___
3 notes ___   6 discussion ___

a gives information about the company (its objectives, products etc.)
b customers' opinions of holidays
c shows other sites that the company thinks are of interest
d shows photos from the holidays
e shows people's opinions
f gives information about new offers and products

Tip!
When evaluating a Facebook page:

- Think about the features on the page.
- Does the page help you understand the holidays *Nordic Visitor* offers?
- Does the page make you want to take a holiday with them? Why/Why not?
- What else would you like to see on the page? Is anything missing, in your opinion?

Remember that when a company keeps a Facebook page, they want you to see them in a very positive light. They includes photos and comments that are positive because they usually want to sell you something.

5 Evaluate the *Nordic Visitor* page's features. Write a short review of the page.

The discussion section is not very useful because it is empty!

Review
In this task I have:

- **explored and evaluated a social networking site**
- **written a short paragraph about a company social networking site.**

CAREERS

Task: Find a summer holiday job in the UK
Tools: UK Summer job websites www.summer-jobs.co.uk   www.summerjobs.co.uk
Skills: Exploring, comparing and evaluating the search function on two websites

Before you start

1 **What would be your ideal summer holiday job? Make notes about:**

- Where you would like to work, e.g. city or country; indoors or outdoors
- What you would like to do
- Full-time or part-time work?
- Live at the place you work or live at home?
- How much you would like to earn

2 **Make a checklist by noting down the answers to the questions above and anything else you would want to know about a job before applying for it.**

Research

3 **Go to the two websites below and try to find a job similar to your ideal job.**

Website 1: **www.summer-jobs.co.uk**   Website 2: **www.summerjobs.co.uk**

Follow these steps with each website.

- Explore the Home page and use the search or browse options to find out about summer jobs
- When you find a job that sounds good, click on the job, or follow the links to the job
- Make notes about the job, using your checklist from Exercise 2

Tip!
Each of these websites gives you a different way to search for a job. Website 1 uses a keyword search, and also allows you to look at job categories on the right. Website 2 asks you to put in search criteria (e.g. country, region and age).

4 **Write a short paragraph describing the job you chose. Give your paragraph to the other students in your class to read.**

Task

5 **Use the table below to help you evaluate and compare the two websites that you used.**

	Website 1	Website 2
Was the home page attractive?		
Was it easy to explore the site from the Home page?		
Was it possible to do a keyword search?		
If you did a keyword search, was it successful? Why/Why not?		
Was it possible to find all the information you wanted about the job? How easy was it?		

Which was the better website in your opinion? Why?

Review
In this task I have:
- written a short paragraph about an ideal summer job
- compared and evaluated searching on two websites.

INNOVATION

Task: Learn about innovations in the field of robots and robotics

Tools: www.youtube.com   www.tubechop.com

Skills: Extracting information from a video and evaluating products shown on videos

Before you start

① **Read the sentences about robots and robotics. Which ones do you agree with?**

1 The world needs more robots.

2 Robots can do many things, but they will never have feelings.

3 In the future, humans will not have to do dirty or dangerous jobs – robots can do them.

4 Robotics has given us many of the best inventions of the last twenty years.

5 Robots can do useful jobs, like cleaning the house or looking after your grandparents.

Research

② **Go to the websites below and watch the videos about robot innovations. As you watch the videos, complete the table below. Tick (✓) if the robot is able to do the task, cross (✗) if the robot is not able to do the task and (?) if the information is not available.**

Robot 1: www.tubechop.com/watch/189385

Robot 2: www.youtube.com/watch?v=eTq16Pbad9o &feature=related

Robot 3: www.tubechop.com/watch/189395 www.tubechop.com/watch/189398

	Robot 1	Robot 2	Robot 3
Speak			
Walk/move horizontally			
Move vertically			
Play games			
Make precise movements			
Communicate			
Clean			
Make noise			

Robot vacuum cleaner

Tip!

If the video isn't playing well, click on the pause symbol and wait for it to load. Once the video has loaded, you can watch the clip without it stopping.

Task

③ **Use the table in Exercise 2 to write a short paragraph explaining which of the robotic inventions in the video clips you think is the most useful and why.**

Review

In this task I have:
• researched robots and their uses
• watched videos about robots
• written a paragraph about robots.

Topic Wordlist

COUNTRY AND SOCIETY

crime and law
arrest (v)
CCTV (n)
criminal (n)
evidence (n)
gun (n)
hijack (v)
illegal (adj)
mugger (n)
murder (v)
pistol (n)
prison (n)
punish (v)
rob (v)
robber (n)
self-defence (n)
violence (n)
violent (adj)

national identity
flag (n)
identity (n)
landmark (n)
language (n)
national anthem (n)
sports team (n)
traditional costume (n)

places
castle (n)
cathedral (n)
farm (n)
skate park (n)
sky-scraper (n)
tube station (n)

politics
apartheid (n)
army (n)
campaign (n)
child labour (n)
civil service (n)
colonialism (n)
communist (adj)
democratic (adj)
demonstrate (v)
demonstration (n)
discrimination (n)
election (n)
equal rights (n)

fight against (v)
fight for (v)
freedom of speech (n)
human rights (n)
immigrant (n)
independence (n)
invader (n)
leader (n)
liberator (n)
march (n)
military (adj)
opponent (n)
peace (n)
peaceful (adj)
poverty (n)
protest (n)
racism (n)
rebellion (n)
revolutionary (n)
ruler (n)
slavery (n)
social reformer (n)
soldier (n)
strike (v)
supporter (n)
take part in (v)
terrorist attack (n)
tyranny (n)
war (n)
women's rights (n)

Catholic (adj)
Muslim (adj)
saint (n)

CULTURE

art
art installation (n)
draw (v)
drawing (n)
modern art (n)
oil painting (n)
paint (v)
painting (n)
sculpture (n)
watercolour (n)
work/piece of art (n)

artists
choreographer (n)
composer (n)
film director (n)
musician (n)

novelist (n)
painter (n)
photographer (n)
playwright (n)
poet (n)
scriptwriter (n)
sculptor (n)
songwriter (n)

describing art
amazing (adj)
awful (adj)
brilliant (adj)
disturbing (adj)
dull (adj)
entertaining (adj)
funny (adj)
good fun (n)
inspiring (adj)
moving (adj)
original (adj)
shocking (adj)
spectacular (adj)
surrealist (adj)
weird (adj)

events
ballet (n)
classical (adj)
concert (n)
contemporary dance performance (n)
exhibition (n)
film (n)
musical (n)
opera (n)
play (n)

literature
fiction (n)
novel (n)
poem (n)
short story (n)

mass media
celebrity (n)
fame (n)
gossip (n)
journalist (n)
magazine (n)
paparazzi (n)
role model (n)
super fan (n)
superstar (n)
TV talk show (n)
website (n)

music
band (n)
boy band (n)
celebrity singer (n)
compose music (v)
greatest hits album (n)
hit song (n)
lead guitarist (n)
music industry (n)
musician (n)
orchestra (n)
sing in a choir (v)
singer (n)
song (n)
song lyrics (n)
symphony (n)

places
art gallery (n)
cinema (n)
museum (n)
theatre (n)

talent shows
applaud (v)
audience (n)
contest (n)
criticize (v)
fan (n)
judge (n)
musician (n)
performer (n)
talent (n)

television, film and theatre
act (v)
actor (n)
actress (n)
advertising ((n))
cartoon (n)
cast (n)
choreography (n)
clip (n)
dancer (n)
director (n)
lead actor (n)
London musical (n)
musical (n)
play (n)
plot (n)
script (n)
set (n)
soap opera (n)
special effect (n)
storyline (n)
theatre critics (n)
West End musical (n)

types of music
alternative (adj)
heavy metal (n)
pop music (n)
rock music (n)

FAMILY AND SOCIAL LIFE

leisure time
barbeque (n)
chess (n)
choir (n)
cookery (n)
dancing (n)
debating club (n)
film club (n)
painting (n)
party (n)
photography (n)
poetry club (n)
riding (n)
roller coaster (n)
school magazine (n)
skateboarding (n)
take photos (v)
trek (n)
voluntary work (n)
write poems (v)

life stages
childhood (n)
divorced (adj)
nursery school (n)

personal/family events
anniversary (n)
birth (n)
celebrate (v)
death (n)
funeral (n)
give birth (v)
invitation (n)
wedding (n)

weddings
best man (n)
bride (n)
bridesmaid (n)
civil ceremony (n)
groom (n)
marry (v)
registry office (n)

FOOD

cooking
bake (v)
boiled (adj)
chef (n)
cook (v)
cookbook (n)
defrost (v)
freeze (v)
fried (adj)
grilled (adj)
ingredient (n)
recipe (n)
roast (adj)
smoked (adj)
stir (v)

describing food and drink
aromatic (adj)
bitter (adj)
creamy (adj)
crispy (adj)
crunchy (adj)
cuisine (n)
delicious (adj)
dessert (n)
disgusting (adj)
fattening (adj)
first course (n)
fizzy (adj)
flavour (n)
fresh (adj)
frozen (adj)
good/bad for you (phrase)
home-made (adj)
main course (n)
medium (adj)
nutritious (adj)
organic (adj)
rare (adj)
raw (adj)
ready-made (adj)
smooth (adj)
soft (adj)
sour (adj)
spicy (adj)
starter (n)
sugary (adj)
sweet (adj)
taste (v)
taste (n)
vegetarian (adj)
well-done (adj)

food items
almond (n)
apple pie (n)
bacon and eggs (n)
beef (n)
cake (n)
cereal (n)
chicken (n)
chip butty (n)
chocolate (n)
cocoa bean (n)
coconut (n)
curry (n)
dairy product (n)
dark chocolate ice cream (n)
egg (n)
fish (n)
fish and chips (n)
fruit (n)
herb (n)
kebab (n)
meat (n)
milk (v)
omelette (n)
seafood (n)
snack (n)
sorbet (n)
steak (n)
sushi (n)
tapas (n)
vegetable (n)

places to eat out
café (n)
coffeehouse (n)
fast-food bar (n)
Indian (adj)
Japanese (adj)
pizzeria (n)
self-service (adj)
take-away (n)
Thai (adj)

HEALTH

healthcare and treatment
aspirin (n)
bacteria (n)
cure (v)
disinfect (v)
first aid (n)
penicillin (n)
surgery (n)
transplant (n)

healthy/unhealthy lifestyle
aerobics (n)
alcohol (n)
calorie (n)
calorie-free (adj)
carbohydrate (n)
drug (n)
drunk (adj)
fat (n)
fibre (n)
lifestyle (n)
mineral (n)
protein (n)
salt (n)
sugar (n)
vitamin (n)
work out (v)

illness/injury
ache (v)
allergy (n)
depression (n)
diabetes (n)
disease (n)
epilepsy (n)
immune system (n)
injure (v)
mental illnesses (n)
skin cancer (n)
suffer (v)

HOUSE

describing a house
air-conditioning (n)
apartment (n)
bedroom (n)
bungalow (n)
camper van (n)
carpet (n)
central heating (n)
cosy (adj)
cottage (n)
detached (adj)
downstairs (adj)
dream (adj)
fireplace (n)
flat (n)
games room (n)
garden (n)
hut (n)
lawn (n)
motor home (n)
outside (adj)

pond (n)
roof (n)
semi-detached (adj)
space (n)
staircase (n)
terrace (n)
terraced (adj)
two-bedroom (adj)
upstairs (adj)
view (n)
warm (adj)

furniture and appliances
cupboard (n)
dishwasher (n)
freezer (n)
fridge (n)
home cinema (n)
oven (n)
sink (n)
sofa (n)
wardrobe (n)
washing machine (n)

housework
chore (n)
iron (v)
mow (v)
tidy (v)

location
busy (adj)
centre (n)
country (n)
downtown ad(v)
outskirts (n)
street (n)
suburb (n)
village (n)

NATURAL ENVIRONMENT

animals
chimpanzee (n)
horse (n)
insect (n)
kangaroo (n)
mosquito (n)
polar bear (n)
rat (n)
seal (n)
shark (n)

snail (n)
whale (n)
wildlife (n)

climate
desert (adj)
dry (adj)
equatorial (adj)
extreme (adj)
Mediterranean (adj)
mild (adj)
rainwater (n)
semi-desert (adj)
storm (n)
subtropical (adj)
temperate (adj)
temperature (n)
tropical (adj)
wet (adj)

environmental issues
air pollution (n)
climate change (n)
CO2 emissions (n)
consumption (n)
deforestation (n)
desertification (n)
destroy (v)
endangered (adj)
exhaust fumes (n)
extinct (adj)
extinction of species (phrase)
extreme weather (n)
flooding (n)
forest fire (n)
litter (n)
nature (n)
noise pollution (n)
nuclear disaster (n)
pollution (n)
recycle (v)
reduce (v)
renewable energy (n)
resistant (adj)
re-use (v)
save energy (v)
share a car (v)
smog (n)
solar panel (n)
solar power (n)
traffic (n)
traffic jam (n)
use public transport (v)
walk (v)
water pollution (n)

wave-powered (adj)
wind farm (n)
wind turbine (n)

landscape
beach (n)
canyon (n)
cliff (n)
coast (n)
desert (n)
forest (n)
hill (n)
jungle (n)
lake (n)
marsh (n)
mountain (n)
palm tree (n)
plain (n)
rainforest (n)
rapids (n)
sea (n)
seaside (n)
stream (n)
valley (n)
waterfall (n)

natural disasters
earthquake (n)
flood (n)
forest fire (n)
hurricane (n)

PEOPLE

appearance
attractive (adj)
beard (n)
blonde hair (n)
brown hair (n)
curly hair (n)
cute (adj)
fair hair (n)
freckle (n)
glamorous (adj)
glasses (n)
good-looking (adj)
gorgeous (adj)
grey hair (n)
handsome (adj)
long hair (n)
moustache (n)
muscular (adj)
nice-looking (adj)
overweight (adj)
piercing (n)

plump (adj)
pretty (adj)
red hair (n)
scruffy (n)
shaved head (n)
short (adj)
short hair (n)
skinny (adj)
slim (adj)
straight hair (n)
stunning (adj)
tall (adj)
tattoo (n)
ugly (adj)
unattractive (adj)
wavy hair (n)
well-built (adj)
well-dressed (adj)
wrinkle (n)

clothes
anorak (n)
badge (n)
baggy (adj)
baseball cap (n)
casual (adj)
colourful (adj)
dark (adj)
designer (adj)
designer label (n)
dinner jacket (n)
elegant (adj)
evening dress (n)
fashion-conscious (adj)
flared (adj)
formal (adj)
good quality (adj)
imaginative (adj)
jeans (n)
kilt (n)
leather jacket (n)
logo (n)
old-fashioned (adj)
overcoat (n)
scarf (n)
smart (adj)
stocking (n)
suit (n)
sweater (n)
trendy (n)
T-shirt (n)

describing people
aristocratic (adj)
intellectual (adj)
middle-class (adj)
poor (adj)
privileged (adj)
royal (adj)
wealthy (adj)
well-known (adj)
well-off (adj)
working class (adj)

feelings and emotions
emotional (adj)
frightened (adj)
petrified (adj)
scared (adj)
stressed (adj)
terrified (adj)
wiped out (adj)

personal qualities
adventurous (adj)
bossy (adj)
competitive (adj)
confident (adj)
creative (adj)
dynamic (adj)
easy-going (adj)
energetic (adj)
friendly (adj)
hard-working (adj)
honest (adj)
idealistic (adj)
impatient (adj)
independent (adj)
keen (adj)
laid-back (adj)
lively (adj)
loyal (adj)
nationalistic (adj)
noisy (adj)
optimistic (adj)
outdoor (adj)
outgoing (adj)
passionate (adj)
practical (adj)
proud (adj)
rebellious (adj)
relaxed (adj)
romantic (adj)
sensitvive (adj)
serious (adj)
shy (adj)
sociable (adj)

sporty (adj)
strict (adj)
untidy (adj)

urban tribes
emo (n)
geek (n)
goth (n)
hippie (adj)
metal head (n)
punk (n)
skater (n)

SCHOOL

learning and exams
academic (adj)
assess my progress (v)
assessment (n)
concentrate in class (v)
concentration (n)
education (n)
examination (n)
learning ability (n)
memorise (v)
memory test (n)
organise my learning (v)
pass an exam (v)
present work neatly (v)
solve problems (v)
work in teams (v)
work online (v)

people and places
assembly hall (n)
comprehensive school (n)
computer lab (n)
elementary school (n)
exchange student (n)
gym (n)
high school (n)
language lab (n)
library (n)
middle school (n)
mixed (adj)
primary school (n)
public school (n)
science lab (n)
secondary school (n)
single-sex (adj)
sixth-form college (n)
sports hall (n)
state school (n)
theatre (n)

school subjects
art and design (n)
business studies (n)
chemistry (n)
citizenship (n)
drama (n)
economics (n)
English language (n)
English literature (n)
geography (n)
ICT (n)
philosophy (n)
physical education (n)
politics (n)
religious education (n)
technology (n)

SCIENCE AND TECHNOLOGY

computer games
avatar (n)
multiplayer (n)
role-playing (adj)
virtual (adj)

describing science and/or technology
breed (v)
crop (n)
gene (n)
gene therapy (n)
genetically modified (adj)
test tube (n)

forensics
analysis (n)
archaeologist (n)
bone (n)
DNA (n)
forensic expert (n)

research areas
artificial intelligence (n)
bio-technology (n)
genetic engineering (n)
nanotechnology (n)
robotics (n)
space travel (n)
virtual reality (n)

sciences

anthropology (n)
archaeology (n)
architecture (n)
astronomy (n)
biology (n)
botany (n)
chemistry (n)
ecology (n)
economics (n)
engineering (n)
genetics (n)
geography (n)
geology (n)
medicine (n)
meteorology (n)
physics (n)
psychology (n)
zoology (n)

space/universe

planet (n)
solar system (n)

technology

abacus (n)
cloning (n)
computer (n)
digital (adj)
gadget (n)
microchip (n)
mobile phone (n)
projector (n)
robot (n)
satellite (n)
screen (n)

using the internet

blog (n)
chat (v)
high-speed internet access (n)
instant messaging (n)
virtual (adj)
wi-fi (n)

SHOPPING AND SERVICES

selling/buying

cash (n)
credit card (n)
customer (n)
dozen (n)
get money back (phrase)

order (v)
pay (v)
receipt (n)
refund (n)
tip (n)

SPORT

sporting events

championship (n)
cheer (v)
crowd (n)
cup final (n)
extra time (n)
goal (n)
medal (n)
prize (n)
race (n)
score (v)
trophy (n)
victory (n)

SPORTS

adventure sports

(rock) climbing (n)
BASE jumping (n)
BMX riding (n)
bungee jump (n)
canoe safari (n)
canoeing (n)
canyoning (n)
caving (n)
extreme skiing (n)
freefall (n)
high lining (n)
kayaking (n)
motorbike (n)
parachuting (n)
scuba diving (n)
sea kayaking (n)
ski jumping (n)
skydiving (n)
snowboarding (n)
surfing (n)
trekking (n)
ultra-light plane (n)
white-water rafting (n)
zip-line (n)

types of sport

cricket (n)
judo (n)
rugby (n)
sailing (n)

TRAVELLING AND TOURISM

holidays

accommodation (n)
backpack (n)
backpacking (n)
camera (n)
camping (n)
cruise (n)
five-star (adj)
guest (n)
hiking (n)
hostel (n)
luggage (n)
opening times (n)
passport (n)
pool (n)
reception (n)
receptionist (n)
resort (n)
snorkelling (n)
souvenir (n)

means of transport

bicycle (n)
boat (n)
helicopter (n)
hitch-hike (v)
plane (n)
underground (n)
yacht (n)

transport

bike lane (n)
bus lane (n)
commuter (n)
congestion charge (n)
four-wheel-drive (n)
public transport (n)
road hump (n)
speed camera (n)
speed limit (n)

WORK

career areas
art and design (n)
business (n)
construction (n)
education (n)
engineering (n)
farming (n)
fashion (n)
finance (n)
industry (n)
law (n)
medicine (n)
politics (n)
science (n)
security (n)
show business (n)
sport (n)
the media (n)
tourism (n)

describing jobs and skills
course (n)
degree (n)
experience (n)
experienced (adj)
field (n)
interview (v)
part-time (adj)
qualification (n)
summer job (n)
well-paid (adj)
work experience (n)

jobs
artist (n)
businessman (n)
businesswoman (n)
cleaner (n)
comedian (n)
dealer (n)
detective (n)
engineer (n)
explorer (n)
farmer (n)
fashion designer (n)
journalist (n)
lawyer (n)
life guard (n)
marine biologist (n)
mechanic (n)
model (n)
police officer (n)

psychologist (n)
psychotherapist (n)
researcher (n)
scientist (n)
shop assistant (n)
sociologist (n)
surgeon (n)
technician (n)
tour guide (n)
writer (n)

money
account (n)
bank details (n)
debt (n)
finance (v)
payment (n)
personal finance (n)
salary (n)

Exam Choice Audioscripts

Exam Choice 1, Listening, exercise 3

Today on *Living Languages*, we are going to look at some of the musicians and bands who choose to sing in minority languages rather than in English, French, German or any other national languages. To help them, an organisation called Liet International organises the Liet song festival each year. The winners of the 2009 festival were SomBy from the Sami area of northern Finland. They sang in Sami, although that isn't as simple as it sounds. There are ten Sami languages and speakers of one cannot always understand speakers of the other nine. The numbers of speakers of the Sami languages are decreasing in Norway, Sweden, Finland and Russia, and these languages are in real danger of disappearing. Perhaps SomBy can help to stop that happening. Amazingly, SomBy are the fourth Sami winners of the competition in the last eight years. The average age of the five members of the band is just eighteen years of age with the oldest member being only twenty. The group sang the rock song *Li Idit Vel* or rather, their singer, Miira Suomi, sang.

To get to the final of the Liet festival, bands take part in local festivals. The Nos Ur, or New Style festival, is for minority speakers in the British Isles as well as Brittany, an area of north-western France. Bands taking part in the festival spoke Scottish Gaelic, Irish Gaelic, Cornish and Welsh and played a variety of musical styles. There was Gaelic rock, Breton rap and Cornish punk. The two winners were Scottish rock band, Sunrise Not Secular, whose good looks made them very popular with the girls watching, and an Irish singer called Fiach.

At the same time, there was another festival called Nos Og, which means Young Style. In fact, although the bands are young, they aren't much different in age to most of the Nos Ur bands. There were three bands playing and, again, there was a mixture of styles. Fionaar were a Scottish rock band, The Stilletoes were Welsh punks and there was a more traditional sound from Irish band, The Temporary. What makes this Nos Og different to Nos Ur is that there is no competition, it's just a concert to enjoy, so the bands are more relaxed and the performances often even better because of that.

We can now listen to Sunrise Not Secular's new CD and then they will be here to talk to me about their music and the Liet festival,

Exam Choice 1, Speaking, exercise 4

Examiner: What do you think of international sports competitions?

A: Well, the biggest are the Olympics but I'm not really interested in them.

B: Neither am I. They're really boring. I love football, though.

A: So do I. Especially the cup final. I'm very excited about the Wimbledon tennis championships this year, too.

B: So am I. I hope the British players do well this time.

Examiner: What environmental problems are you worried about?

A: We have had floods near our house so I'm worried about them.

B: I'm not. We don't live near a river so we're safe. We get a lot of pollution from traffic, though.

Examiner: Do you take an interest in the world's problems?

A: No, I'm not interested in disasters in other countries.

B: I am. I always try to do something to help.

Examiner: Are you interested in the lives of famous people at all?

A: I sometimes read about them in newspapers and magazines but I never watch funerals or weddings of famous people.

B: Neither do I. I can't understand why anyone is interested.

Examiner: What are your favourite days?

A: I guess my birthday is the most important to me. I always have a big party.

B: I don't. I never celebrate my birthday but I like other people's.

A: Why don't you celebrate your birthday?

B: I don't want to grow old.

A: I do, well, not old but I can't wait until I'm old enough to get a job and start earning some money.

Exam Choice 1, Speaking, exercise 5

Examiner: What do you think of international sports competitions?

A: Well, the biggest are the Olympics but I'm not really interested in them.

B: Me neither. They're really boring. I love football, though.

A: Me too. Especially the cup final. I'm very excited about the Wimbledon tennis championships this year, too.

B: Me too. I hope the British players do well this time.

Examiner: What environmental problems are you worried about?

A: We have had floods near our house so I'm worried about them.

B: I'm not. We don't live near a river so we're safe. We get a lot of pollution from traffic, though.

Examiner: Do you take an interest in the world's problems?

A: No, I'm not interested in disasters in other countries.

B: I am. I always try to do something to help.

Examiner: Are you interested in the lives of famous people at all?

A: I sometimes read about them in newspapers and magazines but I never watch funerals or weddings of famous people.

B: Neither do I. I can't understand why anyone is interested.

Examiner: What are your favourite days?

A: I guess my birthday is the most important to me. I always have a big party.

B: I don't. I never celebrate my birthday but I like other people's.

A: Why don't you celebrate your birthday?

B: I don't want to grow old.

A: I do, well, not old but I can't wait until I'm old enough to get a job and start earning some money.

Exam Choice 2, Listening, exercises 3 and 4

Today we are talking about environmentally friendly homes and we are going to start by looking at one man and what he has done in his hometown of Huntsville, a small town with a population of about 35,000 which is in east Texas, about a 100 kilometres north of Houston. His name is Dan Phillips, that's P-H-I-L-L-I-P-S. He's now sixty-four years old and has worked in many jobs, including the army and as a dance teacher. Then, in 1997 he had an idea to build houses from recycled materials. Three things gave him the idea. The first was watching children playing with toy building games and how much fun they had. The second was seeing how much rubbish is thrown away, rubbish that could be recycled. Finally, he cares a lot about poor people and wanted to do something to help them. So, he started his own company, Phoenix Commotion, that's spelt P-H-O-E-N-I-X C-O-M-M-O-T-I-O-N, in 1997, and started to build homes for people who didn't have enough money for a normal house. At first, the houses took eighteen months to build but he can now build a house in just six months. Five builders work for Phoenix Commotion but Dan also asks the person who wants the house to help to build it. When they do that, they really feel it is theirs.

About 80 percent of everything he uses to build the houses is recycled. Some of it comes from other builders, other things he finds in the streets or in rubbish bins. He uses anything: bits of old cars, DVDs, broken mirrors and more. The local government likes what he does and has helped him. In 2004, they opened a special area where people can throw away things they don't want anymore. That means that Dan doesn't have to look for them which saves him a lot of time.

There have been some problems. About half of the people who have bought his houses have now sold them or left. This is usually because they have had money problems but some people have also found that their new house can make them a lot of money. Some richer people in the town have bought the houses because they want something a bit different and special. Dan is a bit sad about this but he doesn't mind too much. The people who he has helped have either got a nice new house or have got some money to buy a different house. He knows he could make more money by selling the houses to the rich people himself but he doesn't make them to become rich.

Exam Choice 2, Speaking, exercise 5

A: Good evening. Can I help you?

B: Yes, please. We need a room for the night. Have you got one?

A: Wait a minute … Yes, we have. It's on the tenth floor.

B: That's fine.

A: There isn't a lift. Do you want a hand with your bags?

B: Yes, please. They're very heavy.

A: No problem. Would you like someone to show you around the hotel before you go to your room?

B: Yes, okay. That's a good idea.

A: I can give you a map of the town too if you like. It shows all the restaurants and shops near here.

B: Great, thanks. Er, shall I give you my passport now?

A: No, don't worry. I can look at it later. First, let me show you the dining room. It's open now if you're hungry.

B: Great. We're starving.

Exam Choice 3, Speaking, exercise 3

A: For the next part of the exam, I'd like you to look at two pictures. They show two different heroes. I'd like you to say what you think they did and what kind of people they were.

B: The first picture is of a man. He must be in his mid-fifties. He's wearing a kind of uniform. He's probably a soldier. He looks very strong and not very friendly. There's a desert in the background. Maybe it's Iraq or Afghanistan but it was taken a long time ago, I think.

The second person is a woman. She looks very kind. In the background, I can see a room with children in it. They look very poor. In my opinion, she's probably a nurse or maybe some sort of social reformer helping to stop child labour.

Exam Choice 3, Listening, exercise 4

Rory: Hi, Amy. You look worried. What's wrong?

Amy: Oh, hi Rory. I have to write about a real life hero for a history project. I don't want to write about anyone obvious like Churchill or Napoleon. I've been looking on the internet for ages but I can't find anyone really good to write about.

Rory: How about Douglas Bader?

Amy: Who?

Rory: He was a pilot in the 1930s. He was very sporty. He was very good at rugby and cricket and he enjoyed life. Most of all, he loved flying.

Amy: Did he fly across the Atlantic or something?

Rory: No, nothing like that. He loved flying dangerously and, one day, he crashed. When he woke up in hospital, he found that he had lost both of his legs.

Amy: Oh no! What happened then?

Rory: He got special legs made of wood, I think. The doctors said that he would never be able to walk properly with them but he was very determined. He tried and tried. It took a long time and he fell over a lot but, eventually, he managed to walk again.

Amy: So why is he a hero?

Rory: Well, a few years later, the Second World War started and he wanted to fly again. Everyone said it was impossible. Then, after a year, because so many pilots had been killed, he got his chance. He was a really good pilot and not having real legs didn't matter at all. Then, one day, his plane was shot down over Europe. His legs were stuck but he was able to take them off and jump out. He was caught and taken to a prison camp.

Amy: With no legs?

Rory: Yes, with no legs but the Germans contacted the British and another plane flew over and dropped a new pair of legs for him. As soon as he got them, he tried to escape but he wasn't able to and he stayed there until the war ended. After the war had finished, he came back to England and the country had a special celebration. Hundreds of planes flew over London and Douglas Bader was in the first one, leading all the others.

Amy: Wow. A real hero. I'll look for more information on the internet. Thanks.

Rory: They made a film about him a few years later. I've got it on DVD. It's very old and in black and white but it's such a wonderful story that it doesn't matter.

Amy: Really? Let's watch it. I'll start my work later. Shall I come to your house?

Rory: No, I'll bring it here. Switch off your laptop and make some popcorn. Wow! I can't believe this.

Amy: What?

Rory: You asking to watch a war film. A black and white war film!

Amy: Well, this is work but I want something new with lots of computer effects on Friday evening!

Exam Choice 4, Listening, exercise 3

P: On *Wildlife at One* this month, we've been looking at different kinds of habitats around the world where wildlife and plants are able to live and grow safely. Today, we're looking at an urban forest, that is a forest inside a city. My guest today is Jennifer Elkins who lives and works in Epping Forest, in the north-east of London. Good morning, Jennifer.

G: Good morning.

P: Tell us about Epping Forest and its history.

G: Well, Epping Forest is nineteen kilometres long from north to south and about four kilometres wide. It's not all forest. There are rivers, marshes and areas of grass as well. It became a royal forest in the 12th century. This was a place where the king could go hunting. It stayed a royal forest until 1878 when the City of London became responsible for it. That means that it became a public space. You can't buy land there or build on it. You can't hunt animals or cut down trees. It is protected but anyone can go there to see it.

P: So, how important is it as a habitat for plants and animals?

G: Very. One of the most special things about it is that no one has cut down any trees since 1878 or taken the wood away. So, the trees are now much bigger than in most forests and there is also a lot of dead wood, where trees have fallen over in storms. Many insects live in this dead wood and it is also home to several plants which like dark, wet places.

There are also some bigger animals in the forest. There are several deer and Britain's only poisonous snake. There's also an animal called a muntjac which is a kind of small deer. They come from China and south Asia but, in 1925, a few of them escaped from a zoo and now they live all over southern England.

P: So, it's a protected area but are there any problems?

G: There are a few. Some roads now go through the forest so we have to build fences to stop the deer running onto the roads. The other problem is more surprising. The trees are now so big that it is difficult for sunlight to reach the ground. That means that many of the flowers and plants that grow in light places have died.

P: The forest is open to people. Is it a popular place?

G: Oh yes. It's very popular. A lot of people cycle there or ride horses. Others go walking or running. There is a special walk every year to remember what happened in 1878. It takes place on the third Sunday in September and we get hundreds of people taking part in that. It's a very enjoyable day.

P: Well, thank you very much for telling us all that. I will have to visit the forest one day.

Exam Choice 4, Speaking, exercise 4

Examiner: What issues does the material deal with?

A: I think the material deals with the problems of waste and how we can reduce this by recycling. Don't you agree?

B: Yes, I do. We can see some rubbish bins in the picture. The headline shows what the government is doing to solve the problem and the table shows that the UK has a bigger problem than a lot of other countries.

Examiner: What problems are caused by waste?

B: There are several problems, aren't there?

A: Yes, there are. There's litter in the streets, the problem of where to put rubbish and the fact that recycling can save energy and trees.

Examiner: How can we encourage people to recycle more?

A: It's a difficult problem, isn't it?

B: Yes, it is. I don't think there are enough recycling bins.

A: Neither do I. People don't like carrying their rubbish a long way. But I don't like ideas like making people pay more to throw away their rubbish.

B: I do. I think it's a very good idea.

Examiner: How much do you recycle?

A: I recycle paper, glass and plastic but I should recycle more.

B: Me too. I know it's important but, sometimes, I'm lazy.

Exam Choice 5, Listening, exercises 3 and 4

P: Today on *Business Week*, we're looking at helping people to find work and be successful but with a slight difference. My guest is Roger Daniels. He is a member of the group 'Success for School Students' which gives advice to school students who are looking for part-time work or who are actually working. Roger is in his final year at university and is hoping to become a businessman when he finishes his studies. Good morning, Roger.

G: Good morning.

P: You're very young to be giving advice to school students. Do they listen to you?

G: Yes, I think the fact that we aren't employers and can remember our own school days makes our advice more relevant for a lot of people.

P: So, what exactly does your group do?.

G: A number of things. Of course, we can't go round the country helping individuals but we do give ideas of where to look for work. People who have never worked before often don't think about even quite obvious ideas such as looking in the local newspaper. Once they have found a job, they then often need help with the interview.

P: In what way?

G: Things like what to wear and simple things like having clean shoes or making your hair look nice. As well as looking right, they need to know how to behave, for example waiting to be asked to sit down and looking into the interviewer's eyes when they are talking. People who look away don't look honest. They look as if they are trying to hide something. Probably, they are just very nervous but that's not what the interviewer will think and they will be less likely to get a job. Finally, they need help with what to say. They need to talk about themselves and make their lives and interests sound interesting.

P: How can they do that?

G: Well, extra-curricular activities are a very good thing to put on a CV. The difference between saying 'My interests are computers and films' and saying 'I go to the school's computer club twice a week and also belong to the film club' is huge. They are the same interests but have a different effect on the interviewer.

P: I see what you mean. What about when students are in work. Do they still need help?

G: Oh yes. At school, teachers are always telling you what to do. At work, you often have to be much more independent, work on your own or as part of a team and be able to organise your time yourself.

P: So how do you give this advice? Is there a magazine?

G: No, it's too expensive. We have a website with lots of articles on it and pages where school students can share their experiences and learn from other people's mistakes. Our next plan is to put some videos of good and bad interviews onto the website.

P: That sounds great. Good luck and thank you for coming.

G: Thank you.

Exam Choice 5, Speaking, exercise 6

E: Right, now for the next part of the exam, I'm going to ask you both a few questions about English. First of all, Ela.

A: Er ... is it okay if I have a drink of water?

E: Of course. Is that better? Good. Now, Ela, could you tell me how long you have been studying English?

A: I've been studying English for five years. We started in Year six and I have been going to private lessons for two years.

E: I see. Can you say how you use English outside school?

A: Er, well ...

B: Do you mind if I answer this question?

E: I'm sorry, but these are Ela's questions. I'll ask you in a minute. So, Ela.

A: Well, I read a lot in English and I write a blog in English. I also ...

B: Do you think I could say something, please?

E: In a minute, Hans. Please let Ela finish.

Exam Choice 6, Listening, exercises 3 and 4

P: On *Art Today*, my guest is an expert on abstract and modern art, which is normally the sort of thing I avoid, but I have agreed to look at ten 'classic' art works and learn something about them. Welcome Antonia Fisher.

G: Thank you. I'm sure you'll like these.

P: Let's start with number one.

G: This is Black Square by Kazimir Malevich, a Russian artist and it is a black square. He called this the zero of modern art, like the number zero in maths. The start of everything. So, what do you think?

P: I guess, my main thought is that I could do that. There's no artistic skill to it.

G: A lot of people think like that but it's the idea that is important. Okay, number two is The Snail by Matisse. It's made of pieces of coloured paper stuck down in the shape of a snail's shell.

P: Almost like a snail's shell. This look very much like what my five-year-old son does at school. Perhaps he's a genius too?

G: Perhaps he is! I think you'll like this. It's called On White and it's by Wassily Kandinsky.

P: Ah yes. Now this I like. It looks musical. There aren't any musical instruments but the effect when I look at it is of music. Something like jazz, maybe. I'm not sure why.

G: That's excellent. Kandinsky was a musician as well as an artist. Next is Onement 1 by Barnett Newman.

P: This is a little bit boring. It looks like a piece of wood with a badly painted orange stripe down the middle.

G: Newman called those lines 'zips' and most of his paintings had them.

P: I always think of lines when I think of modern art.

G: Well, the next two paintings will make you happy. The first is Composition 10 by Mondrian.

P: Ah yes, it looks like little metal pipes going from side to side and up and down. It's a bit like a computer game. I quite like this.

G: The next is Counter-Composition five – with a Roman five, like a V – by Theo Van Doesburg.

P: This is very bright with a large red square but I prefer Mondrian's lines.

G: Okay, next we have one by Fernand Leger and it's called Railway Crossing.

P: It's great. It looks very modern with an idea of industry and technology. The only thing I can't see is a railway crossing!

G: It's there. Keep trying. Now, my last painting is Whistler's Black and Gold: The falling rocket. It's a picture of fireworks over the Thames but it's very dark.

P: I love the dark, black smoke. You can almost smell it. It might not look great in a living room but, in a bright art gallery where you can stand back and look at it from a distance, this must be very impressive. Thank you for bringing these. I liked some of them more than I expected.

G: Thank you for inviting me. I'm glad I have been at least half successful.

Exam Choice 6, Speaking, exercise 5

Examiner: What music do you like listening to?

Student: In my opinion, older rock music is better than music made now. For example, some of the songs that The Beatles sang nearly fifty years ago still sound great and fresh when you hear them on the radio. The main reason I like rock music is that there are many different sounds all being played at the same time and you hear something different each time you listen. Another reason I like it is that it is good to listen to, good to dance to, good to sing or just to have in the background.

Examiner: Imagine you could have only one song on your MP3 player. What would it be?

Student: I love the classic groups like Pink Floyd, The Doors and Led Zeppelin. I would choose a song by one of them. The song I would choose is *Stairway to Heaven*. The reason for that is that it is a mixture of different styles.

Exam Choice and Online Skills Answer Key

Exam Choice 1

1 1 T 2 F 3 T 4 F 5 F 6 T 7 F 8 F

2 1 Heartwarming - happy 2 Over the moon - very happy 3 Our hearts were in our mouths - we were very nervous 4 It was pointless - there was no reason for it

3 1 b 2 b 3 d 4 c 5 b 6 d

4 2 So do 3 So am 4 not 5 am 6 Neither do 7 don't 8 do

5 1 Me neither 2 Me too 3 Me too 4 ✗ 5 ✗ 6 Me neither 7 ✗ 8 ✗

6 1 c 2 b 3 b 4 a 5 a 6 c 7 b 8 a 9 c 10 a

7 1 fashion-conscious, easy-going, hard-working 2 reading, watching TV, skiing, taking photographs 3 blonde, slim, tall, good-looking 4 actors, like Tom Cruise, Johnny Depp and Ewan McGregor, sports, like basketball, football and hockey, urban tribes, like goths, punks and emos

8 Students' own answers

Exam Choice 2

1 a

2 1 Cornwall / the south-west of England 2 800 years 3 warm/hot 4 the local area 5 kinds of pasties 6 break 7 their hands 8 smaller 9 Spanish

3 Students' own answers

4 1a 100km (north) b 35,000 2a Phillips b He was in the army and was a dance teacher 3a Phoenix Commotion b 1997 c 18 months 4a About 80 percent 5a 2004 5 (About) half of them

5 1 Would Can 5 help hand 7 want like 9 that if 10 Would Shall 11 make let

6 1 was sent 2 case 3 about 4 bit 5 had 6 like me 7 more 8 to have 9 is being 10 hand

7a Students' own answers

7b Students' own answers

8 1 because 2 in case 3 just in case 4 as

9 Students' own answers

Exam Choice 3

1 1 f 2 e 3 a 4 c 5 b 6 d

2 1 f 2 d 3 e 4 a 5 g 6 c

3 1 must 2 kind 3 probably 4 looks 5 background 6 Maybe 7 think 8 In 9 look 10 opinion 11 of

4 1 c 2 a 3 b 4 c 5 a 7 b

5 1 slavery 2 illegal 3 wealthy 4 twenties 5 racism 6 poverty 7 impossible 8 disagreed 9 demonstrations 10 women's

6 1 wants 2 make 3 like 4 to help

7 Students' own answers

Exam Choice 4

1 2 free F 3 finished F 4 checked F 5 value O 6 24 F

2 1 g 2 i 3 a 4 d 5 e 6 c 7 f 8 h

3 1 In the north-east of London 2 19km long and 4km wide 3 In the 12th century 4 The City of London 5 Insects and plants (that like dark, wet places) 6 deer, snakes (muntjac) 7 China and south Asia 8 Roads going through the forest, trees getting too big and stopping the sunlight reaching the ground 9 The third Sunday in September

4 1 agree 2 do 3 there 4 are 5 it 6 Neither 7 do 8 think 9 too

5 1 in 2 of 3 about 4 going 5 diving 6 part 7 be 8 themselves 9 to 10 other

6 1 sending 2 going 3 doing 4 finishing 5 doing

7 Students' own answers

Exam Choice 5

1 1 c 2 f 3 e 4 a 5 b

2 b 5 c 1 d 4 e × f 3

3 a 6 b 3 c 7 d 1 e 4 f 2 g 5

4 1 b 2 c 3 c 4 b 5 a 6 b

5 1 Is it okay if I have a drink of water? 2 Could you tell me how long you have been studying English? 3 Can you say how you use English outside school? 4 Do you mind if I answer this question? 5 Do you think I could say something, please?

6 1 S 2 E 3 E 4 S 5 S

7 1 I was good at 2 difference between 3 get in touch with 4 he had taken 5 me why you would like 6 me how to start 7 comes up with 8 subjects I wanted 9 take care of 10 if my brother belonged

8 1 c 2 a 3 b

9 Students' own answers

Exam Choice 6

1 1 b 2 c 3 d 4 e 5 a

2 1 a 2 c 3 a 4 d 5 c 6 c 7 b

3 1 c 2 g 3 a 4 b 5 e 6 d 7 f 8 h

4 (Suggested answers) 2 It's like what my son does at school 3 It looks musical 4 It's dull, it looks like a piece of wood with a badly painted orange stripe down the middle 5 looks like metal pipes, looks like a computer game 6 Very bright, it has a large red square 7 It looks very modern, ideas of industry and technology, can't see a railway crossing 8 I love it, it would look good in a bright gallery, you can almost smell the smoke

5 1 opinion 2 For 3 main 4 that 5 Another 6 like 7 reason

6 1 b 2 d 3 b 4 a 5 c 6 a 7 c 8 d 9 b 10 d

7 1 although 2 Despite 3 However 4 Although

8 Students' own answers

Online Skills 1

1 1 July and August 2 February 3 Beijing (2008) and London (2012) 4 baseball and water-skiing

Online Skills 2

3 1 Builds and repairs homes for people in need, including improving water and sanitation 2 400,000 3 homeowners and volunteers 4 twenty-two

4 1 one week 2 Nacho is a volunteer from Spain. He says that the experience of volunteering has made him feel good about himself. 3 ArcelorMittal is the partner. It produces steel.

Online Skills 4

3 Students' own answers

4 1 c 2 d 3 f 4 a 5 b 6 e

Online Skills 6

2

	Robot 1	Robot 2	Robot 3
Speak	?	✗	✗
Walk/move horizontally	✓	✓	✓
Move vertically	✓	✗	✓
Play games	?	✗	✓
Make precise movements	✓	✗	✓
Communicate	✓	✗	✓
Clean	✗	✓	✗
Make noise	✓	?	?

Pearson Education Limited
Edinburgh Gate
Harlow
Essex CM20 2JE
England
and Associated Companies throughout the world.

www.pearsonELT.com

© Pearson Education Limited 2012

The right of Rod Fricker to be identified as author of this Work has been asserted by him in accordance with the Copyright, Designs and Patents Act 1988.

First published 2012
Tenth impression 2019
ISBN: 978-1-4082-9615-8
Set in Neo Sans Std 9pt
Printed in Malaysia (CTP-VVP)

Acknowledgements

The publisher would like to thank the following for their kind permission to reproduce their photographs:

(Key: b-bottom; c-centre; l-left; r-right; t-top)

Photo acknowledgements

The publisher would like to thank the following for their kind permission to reproduce their photographs:

(Key: b-bottom; c-centre; l-left; r-right; t-top)

Adam White: Adam White 58tr; **Alamy Images:** Jeffrey Blackler 73tr, Mike Goldwater 76tr, Tim Graham 54cr, Gert Lavsen 116, Photos 12 47, Jack Sullivan 54tl, Vario Images GmbH & Co. KG 54tr, World History Archive 54br, wronaphoto.com 76tl; **Bridgeman Art Library Ltd:** Newell Convers Wyeth / Peter Newark American Pictures 52; **Corbis:** John Bryson / Sygma 54bl, Stephane Cardinale / People Avenue 110, Jorge Ferrari / epa 32, Hulton-Deutsch Collection 50, Robbie Jack 94; **Getty Images:** Ian Gavan 22br, Carlos Hernandez 62tr, Ralf Juergens 22cr, Popperfoto 14/2.3a, 55, David Thompson 22tr, Universal Images Group / Hulton Archive 56; **iStockphoto:** Jani Bryson 79, keeweeboy 62tl, Dale Reardon 36, t-lorien 62tc; **Keith Partridge:** keith Partridge 58tl; **Press Association Images:** Jorge Saenz / AP 18; **Rex Features:** Stephen Simpson 54cl; **Shutterstock.com:** Yuri Arcurs 91, Luminis 20, Radu Razvan 86, Nick Reynolds Photography 73bl; **SuperStock:** Newstockimages 88; **The Kobal Collection:** De Line Pictures 108br, Warner Bros. / David James 113, New Line / David James 108b, Revolution Studios 108cr

Cover images: *Front:* **Alamy Images:** Danita Delimont cl; **Getty Images:** Nick Koudis c, Juliet White cr; **Photolibrary.com:** Image Source r; **Plainpicture Ltd:** Hoch Zwei l

All other images © Pearson Education

Every effort has been made to trace the copyright holders and we apologise in advance for any unintentional omissions. We would be pleased to insert the appropriate acknowledgement in any subsequent edition of this publication.

Illustration acknowledgements

Illustrated by John Batten 5, 31, 33, 69, 103; Kathy Baxendale 13, 25 (r), 39, 65; Bill Piggins 11, 12, 30 (r), 49, 61, 83, 105; Mark Ruffle 15, 30 (l), 43, 48, 51, 67, 97; Sean 087 (KJA Artists) 29, 40, 44, 85, 87; Simon Tegg 3, 4, 21, 32, 57, 101, 104.

Cover images: *Front:* **Alamy Images:** Danita Delimont cl; **Getty Images:** Nick Koudis c, Juliet White cr; **Photolibrary.com:** Image Source r; **Plainpicture Ltd:** Hoch Zweil